W9-BSR-602

Women and the Family
in Rural Taiwan

Margery Wolf

Women and the Family in Rural Taiwan

Stanford University Press
Stanford, California
1972

HQ
1740.5
W6.5

Stanford University Press
Stanford, California
© 1972 by the Board of Trustees of the
Leland Stanford Junior University
Printed in the United States of America
ISBN 0-8047-0808-8
LC 70-183895

To Arthur

368633

ALUMNI MEMORIAL LIBRARY
Creighton University
Omaha, Nebraska 68178

Preface

The wife of an anthropologist finds it nearly impossible not to be something of an anthropologist herself. In the course of my husband's several field trips to Taiwan, I have lived in a variety of places in the Taipei basin: in the capital city of Taipei, with a farm family in a country village, and in a small market town on the edge of the mountains that rim the basin. Unlike the United States, Taiwan is a place where much of life is carried on in full view of the neighbors. Religious ceremonies, marriage processions, and the elaborate rituals of death seem designed to draw crowds of onlookers. In the villages, routine chores are done in the doorway within chatting distance of several neighbors; child-training takes place where the children are, which is to say, outdoors in all but the heaviest rains; and, sooner or later, family conflicts are brought out of the house to be judged by village opinion. It is impossible *not* to make observations and eventually to ask questions about what is observed. Almost without exception, the questions are graciously answered. This book about Taiwanese country women has grown out of these casual observations, some interviewing, and many raids on my husband's field notes. I am greatly indebted to him and to his field staff.

A book by a woman about women in a culture known for its androcentricity is always in danger of becoming a critique of that culture. I have tried to avoid that temptation—with,

I admit, varying degrees of success. Those who feel strongly about the Women's Liberation Movement in the West, pro and con, will no doubt find ample material to support their assertions about the nature of womankind and her relations with her menfolk. As a woman, I cannot be without bias on these issues, but I have tried to control my biases and to label them, when I cannot. I think, however, before the reader dismisses some of the unorthodoxies he finds here as distortions resulting from the sex of the author, he should consider whether they are not the natural result of the theme. Authors, both male and female, select from the totality of life those aspects relevant to their topic. When that topic is China, the perspective has nearly always been male. When the other half of Chinese society is the focus, the "reality" of Chinese social life looks different. If I have done a fair job of presenting that reality for the women of Taiwan, he who finds it distorted must look to his own biases.

The body of the book follows the life cycle of women in rural Taiwan, but the first four chapters are devoted to general background material: a brief historical sketch of the island and a description of the settings in which my observations were made; a chapter describing the history and present situation of a particular family, written with the conventional focus on the male descent group; a brief chapter that presents some of the ideas I have developed in trying to relate Chinese women to the Chinese kinship system; and a short chapter describing the interrelationships among women in the community with which I am most familiar. Although the historical sketch may seem unnecessary, I feel required to include it in order to lay a ghost familiar to those who have studied Taiwanese culture. Taiwan is ethnically Chinese, just as Chinese as Peking is. To be sure, the Taiwanese have customs that differ from those in Peking, but so do the people of Shanghai, and indeed so do the Chinese who live in small villages forty

Preface

miles from Peking. My insistence on the Chineseness of the Taiwanese should in no way be construed as a political statement. The question of who rules Taiwan is a matter that should be decided by those who live there.

Frequently in the pages that follow I will make use of the pronoun "we." This is not the ubiquitous editorial "we." The conversations and interviews from which I quote were recorded by several members of our field staff on different field trips, both independently and in combination with my husband or me. To label each quotation properly would be difficult and in any case would make rather dry reading.

Hokkien words and names are romanized according to the system devised by Nicholas C. Bodman in his text *Spoken Amoy Hokkien* (Charles Grenier & Son, Kuala Lumpur, 1955). Tone marks have been omitted. All personal names and surnames are fictitious, as are the place-names of the village of Peihotien and its market town, Tapu. I owe particular thanks to Margaret Sung (Yan Mian), who stumbled up mountain paths and through paddy fields with me, smiling even after the dreariest of interviews and an encounter with a snake. Even now, many thousands of miles from where we met, she continues to help me with the difficult romanization of Hokkien names. I am also indebted to Don DeGlopper, Roxane Witke, Norma Diamond, and Stevan Harrell for their suggestions.

There are many other people who have helped me, a number of them without realizing that the end product would be this book. The women of Peihotien and Sanhsia rank highest on this list. Some may say I have exploited them. It is certainly true that I took a great deal from them and that they freely gave me a great deal, but they are none the poorer as a result. I do not deny my debt; indeed, it is in recognition of how much I owe them that I have written this book. It is my hope that through the book these women and the many lives they represent will be given a more prominent place in the history of our species. The reader, too, in turning these pages will be exploiting the women of Taiwan and may even come away a richer person as a result of his contact with them; but this is the kind of exploitation that leads to understanding and perhaps to friendship, and hopefully makes us all a little more human.

M.W.

Contents

Women and the Family
in Rural Taiwan

Some History and Some Geography

Taiwan's early history is not unlike that of North America. Portuguese explorers "discovered" the island early in the sixteenth century, and various commercial interests, as well as Japanese and Chinese pirates, laid claim to it for different periods thereafter. The aborigines, a Malayo-Polynesian people, were robbed of their land, their dignity, and often their lives by the Chinese colonists who followed the explorers. They did not submit with docility; well into the twentieth century there was an "aborigine problem." Unwary travelers and forest camphor-workers were prime targets for headhunters, but raids were also conducted against villages on the plains. Taiwan's treacherous shoreline witnessed many shipwrecks, and it early became apparent to pirate and naval captain alike that those who survived the surf rarely survived their first contact with the aborigines. In the nineteenth century the Ching court, which ostensibly governed Taiwan, refused to pay indemnities to countries thus injured and even admitted its inability to control the aborigines. As a result, both Japan and the United States at different times led punitive expeditions onto Taiwan in search of the tribes who had massacred their shipwrecked nationals. Neither country was entirely successful. Today these fierce fighters, like many Indian tribes of North America, are a picture of apathy, living in poverty and squalor in the mountains, defeated less by military might than by alcoholism and the diseases of civilization.

The Chinese culture hero in Taiwan's history is Koxinga (Cheng Ch'eng-kung). Koxinga and his father were pirate-merchants of humble origin who eventually controlled the trade along most of the southeast coast of China. For a few years after the Manchu conquest of China, Koxinga's father remained loyal to the defeated Ming dynasty, but in time he succumbed to offers of rank and autonomy in exchange for token submission. According to some reports, he was captured by trickery soon after and taken to Peking in chains.* His Japanese wife, Koxinga's mother, committed suicide rather than be taken prisoner. Koxinga, who had refused to join his father in submission, became even more determined to reinstate the Ming after this turn of events. He increased his trade (and pirate) activities and with the increased revenue raised an army. After several successes, the army suffered a major defeat when it attacked Nanking, and in 1662 Koxinga was forced to abandon his hold on the South China mainland. Looking to Taiwan for a new base, he drove out the Dutch East India Company, which had been in control since 1623, and took over the island as his own kingdom.

Taiwan's new ruler, who was in many ways its first ruler, put his defenses in order and then set out on a famous tour of his realm. The mythology that quickens the hearts of many children in Tapu and Sanhsia claims this tour took Koxinga as far north as the Taipei basin, where he subdued a great man-eating bird near the town of Yingke and permanently choked off the poisonous vapors emanating from the mountain that overlooks Sanhsia. In fact, Koxinga never seems to have gone much farther north than Taichung, but his status

---

* I lean heavily in this historical section on the old but excellent account of Taiwan's early years by James W. Davidson, *The Island of Formosa: Past and Present* (New York: Macmillan, 1903).

as a culture hero is deserved even if he did not slay monsters. He was an able administrator as well as a skillful diplomat and soldier, and had he not died shortly after his tour, Taiwan's history might have followed a different course. His son ruled ably despite a youthful reputation as a wastrel, but he too died an early death, leaving Taiwan's rule to the vagaries of palace intrigue. The illegitimate son he had carefully trained to succeed him was assassinated, and the eldest of his legitimate sons, aged twelve, was put on the throne. Within a year the boy and his incompetent advisers were forced to submit to the Peking government and hand over the administration of the island to the governor of Fukien.

For the next two hundred years Taiwan was virtually ignored by the Ching government. When attention was called to the island it was only because troops and money were needed from the mainland to put down another of Taiwan's periodic insurrections. Officials sent out to administer the island (as a prefecture of Fukien) knew that their term would be short. They tended to fill their pockets as rapidly as possible and to take little responsibility for the development of the island. The maintenance of order and the upkeep of the few existing roads depended entirely on the local population, and in general the job was too much for them. The Chinese population had continual skirmishes with the aborigines and at the same time were involved in endless disputes within their own ranks. The immigrants from Fukien quarreled with the Kwangtung immigrants. The Fukien settlers came primarily from two small districts near Amoy: Chuanchou to the north and Changchou to the south. Under frontier conditions it was good to have a claim of obligation and loyalty beyond that of kinship, and the theft of a Changchou man's pig by a Chuanchou man might well bring on a battle between large groups called on to protect the rights of their "brother." These same people might another day be redivided when the Ongs and the Lims of Changchou had a falling out over water rights. A short journey of twenty miles was so full of hazards that few attempted it without armed escorts. It is not surprising that the Taiwanese gained a reputation for being quarrelsome and rebellious; they were.

It was not until 1887 that the Ching government recognized the economic and political importance of Taiwan by promoting it to the status of a province. By then Taiwan had a flourishing agricultural economy and a lucrative foreign trade in camphor, tea, sugar, and rice. It needed only improved communications and a stable administration to make it into one of China's most valuable provinces. Liu Ming-chuan, an extraordinarily progressive administrator for his time, was appointed the first governor. He thoroughly reorganized the island's government, moved the capital north to the city of Taipei, paved the capital's streets and lighted them with electricity, took the first census (by 1893 the Chinese population had grown to 2,546,000), laid telegraph cables to join Taiwan to the world's communications, and built the island's first railroad. Not all the projects worked out—the railroad in particular fell prey to graft and technical incompetence—but the most serious failure of Liu's administration concerned the aborigines. He tried to undo several hundred years of brutalization with a border pacification plan. Lowland tribes were paid to till land that lay between the Chinese settlements and the territory of the hill tribes. Unfortunately, both of the militant groups attacked the buffer communities, setting off a new series of even bloodier encounters. The lucrative camphor industry was brought to a virtual halt. This state of affairs did not make Liu popular with either his superiors or the merchants, or for that matter with the common people. Even worse, to pay for his many improvements he had to devise new means of taxation, and his reorganized administration put into important positions more mandarins who required

4

more payoffs. There was so much hostility toward Liu that he did not dare travel in some districts on the island. When he retired in 1891, his successor made few attempts to carry on his progressive plans.

In 1895, at the conclusion of the Sino-Japanese War, Taiwan was ceded to the Japanese, who spent the better part of the next year trying to take possession of their new colony. The Taiwanese had no genuinely nationalistic feelings to weld them into a resistance force of any power, but the ragtag private armies of some wealthy men, bands of robbers, and the usual Chinese hostility toward any outsider combined to provide the Japanese troops with considerably more harassment than they had anticipated. Even so, the Japanese suffered the majority of their casualties from the diseases endemic to the island.*

During the next fifty years, the Chinese population of Taiwan was under the administration of the Japanese government. Although fifty years is little more than the life span of one islander, some scholars imply that it was sufficient to destroy the essence of a culture several thousand years old. It is true that the Japanese had a remarkable effect on the stability, economy, health, and communications of Taiwan. However, it should be noted that the new rulers made intensive studies of Taiwanese customary law in order to properly enforce it, not destroy it. Intermarriage with Japanese was prohibited until 1932; taking a Japanese name was not allowed until 1942; education in Japanese schools was not encouraged, and college education was limited to training doctors and public health workers. The advantages of making loyal Japanese

---

* Harry J. Lamley has written an interesting paper on this war: "The 1895 Taiwan War of Resistance: Local Chinese Efforts Against a Foreign Power," in Leonard H. D. Gordon, ed., *Taiwan: Studies in Chinese Local History* (Occasional Papers of the East Asian Institute, Columbia University, 1970).

citizens out of Taiwan's population evidently were not considered seriously until the 1930's. Whether they wished it or not, the Taiwanese were given little opportunity to acquire the values or the modes of Japanese culture. The Taiwanese probably spoke and read more Japanese during the 1950's than they ever did under Japanese rule, but they clearly did so as a form of social protest, a statement of disappointment. It may have been on the basis of observations made during this period that foreign observers (and some Chinese) reached their mistaken conclusions about the influence of Japanese culture on the Chinese population of Taiwan.

When Taiwan was handed back to the Chinese in 1945, the economy was viable, if shaky. Under the Japanese, the Taiwanese had come to assume certain standards of efficiency, health, justice, and living. The military government imposed by the infamous Chen Yi, the brutal mass murders of Taiwanese leaders and potential leaders after the 1947 rebellion, and the systematic looting of the country's industry left the island far worse off than it had been during the war, Allied bombing raids notwithstanding. When Chiang Kai-shek arrived with one million refugees in 1949, the Taiwanese population had been transformed from the naïve welcoming kinsmen of 1945 to resentful subjects. After twenty years some of the wounds inflicted in this bitter period (by both sides) have healed, but the scars are almost as painful and certainly as apparent as the original wounds.

Thanks to the Joint Commission on Rural Reconstruction, an effective and honest organization and an admirable example of Sino-American cooperation, great strides have been made in strengthening the economy of Taiwan—but the basis for this economic success was laid by the Japanese. They provided the farmers of Taiwan with major agricultural innovations, not the least of which was the island's large, complicated irrigation system; they built the railroad; they brought electricity even to the remote villages (a source of great amazement to arriving mainlanders, some of whose country relatives had never so much as seen an electric light); and they began the industrialization of Taiwan. Obviously, the Japanese development was not altruistic, and much of it ceased during the later years of the war. But the foundations were laid. It is easier to repair or rebuild neglected or bombed-out factories and railroads than to design new ones from scratch. To maintain or even replace a communications system once it has been established is quite different from creating such a system. And anyone acquainted with Taiwanese farmers knows they would not revert to less productive farming methods unless they had no choice. When the Nationalists took over the island, they found an economy weakened both by the immense strains the Japanese put on it during the closing years of the war and by the irresponsible usage it had received in the 1945–49 period, but an economy still capable of recovery. Thanks to the impartial guidance of the Joint Commission, American aid, and the capacity of the Taiwanese for hard work, Taiwan in the last twenty years has been able to absorb the additional strain of a massive government bureaucracy and has almost managed to return to its prewar position of maintaining the second highest standard of living in the Far East. It probably has more to fear now from its skyrocketing population than from any other single problem. The government, far more conservative than the farmers, has finally allowed a rational birth control program to replace the illegal abortion mills that maimed so many women. In spite of the people's strong values on having many sons, the Taiwanese have accepted the program eagerly. As early as 1958 the unsophisticated women I knew in Peihotien were aware of the seriousness of the problem in their own families. They were ready for help (and asking foreigners like us for it) long before it was available.

This, then, is a too brief outline of the past of a young nation with a long history. I present it so the reader may place the chapters that follow in some context, and to clarify once again the origin and culture of the people of Taiwan. Taiwan was a frontier province of China, and as such was no more or no less cut off from the mainstream of Chinese life than any other frontier province. The fact that Taiwan is an island was no more a detriment to its relations with the rest of China than some of China's mountain ranges are to other provinces. The mainland city of Amoy was, after all, one of Taiwan's markets for fresh pork and garden produce. Taiwanese unity—nationalism, if you will—developed during the island's years as a colony of Japan, but there remain important differences within its population. Like the rest of China, Taiwan is ethnically diverse. Hokkien-speakers, whose ancestors came from Fukien province, distinguish themselves from Hakka, the Chinese immigrants who traditionally have arrived on the last wave of every migration and eked out a living on the poorest land. (In Taiwan they fared considerably better.) The majority of Taiwan's population are Hokkien-speakers, and I follow the custom in this book that justifiably irritates the Hakka and the anthropologists who study them: I use the term Taiwanese to refer to Hokkien-speakers. "Mainlander" is the term I use for those from other provinces who immigrated after the fall of the mainland.

The Tamsui, a major river twisting and turning through the Taipei basin, provides one of the borders of the city of Taipei. Many miles upstream, on one of the river's many bends, is the village of Peihotien. Here my husband and I spent two years living with a farm family, studying the subjects that attract anthropologists to remote villages in distant countries. In summer it would have been difficult to find a more comfortable place to live in Taiwan. The nearby river

8

gave at least the impression of coolness, and plentiful shade trees gave some truth to the semblance. The Lim family with whom we lived had (like most of their neighbors) an old-fashioned brick farmhouse with thick walls and a steep tile roof—perfect protection from tropical summer sun. In winter Peihotien was no more uncomfortable than any other village in northern Taiwan. The temperature in this area rarely goes below freezing, but the endless rain creates a damp chill that permeates everything. The only source of heat in country homes comes from the brick cooking stoves, and they are fired at most twice a day.

In 1959 the population of Peihotien was approximately five hundred people. At that time the majority of the families owned some farmland and derived at least a part of their income from the land. The nearby market town of Tapu and the larger towns closer to Taipei had small industries that provided jobs for many of the younger men of Peihotien and those of the unmarried girls whose parents allowed them to work outside the village. Although Taipei was less than an hour's trip away (half by foot and half by train), there were two old ladies in the village who claimed with apparent pride that they had never been there. A good many of the children made their first visit to the city as part of a school outing in the fifth or sixth grade.

When we returned to Taiwan in 1968 for a much shorter stay, I found many things changed. The oxcarts and pedicabs were gone from Taipei's streets, and the skyline was totally altered by the many-storied Western-style hotels and office buildings. Tapu, the market town nearest Peihotien, has expanded beyond recognition, with rows of ugly apartment houses filling the once open fields. Unfortunately, prosperity and change have scarred the tranquility of Peihotien too. Its proximity to Taipei made it an ideal spot to raise chickens, both for market and for egg production. Many of the iridescent paddy fields have been filled with square ugly chicken houses. The sight and sound of new construction is everywhere. Even in the heart of Peihotien there are several new concrete bungalows. To the foreigner, these shoddy imitations of Western architecture look pathetic next to the dignified lines of a traditional brick farmhouse, but to the Taiwanese they look chic and modern. Most of Peihotien's big trees have been destroyed either by storms or by construction. The magnificent old tree that sheltered Peihotien's shrine for Tho-te-kong (the god of the land) went down in the disastrous typhoon and flood of 1963. With it disappeared the essence of a country village.

In 1968 we lived again in the Taipei basin and again on the banks of a river, but not in Peihotien. This time we stayed in the small market town of Sanhsia on the very edge of the Taipei basin at the foot of the mountains. As the crow flies, we were only five miles from our former residence, and some of our new neighbors were relatives of our old ones. Nearly all were the descendants of immigrants from Anchi, a small section of the Chuanchou district in Fukien. Sanhsia, like Peihotien's market town of Tapu, provides services and a daily market for the small villages and isolated farms around it, but unlike Tapu it has not been overwhelmed by the changes of the last decade. The railroad does not pass through Sanhsia, and the highway that leads to it disintegrates on the other side of town into a number of small unpaved roads traveled mainly by creaky old buses, long since retired from the major bus companies. In the last century Sanhsia was an important river port, receiving camphor wood and tea from the mountains and shipping these products downstream to the sea. Most of its growth dates from this phase of its history. Where Tapu has whole neighborhoods of Japanese houses, Sanhsia has remodeled farmhouses and a lovely street of old-fashioned Chinese business establishments. The commercial district has moved away from what is still known as Shop Street to more modern establishments, but the sober timbers of the unpainted shop fronts still open onto the street, disclosing to the curious the long, narrow series of rooms and courtyards behind. At present much of the construction in Sanhsia is reconstruction. The market burned down soon after our arrival, and reconstruction was started shortly before we left. The other major building job in Sanhsia is the slow, loving renovation of the Co-su-kong temple, a task that has been going on for twenty years.

To many young Taiwanese Sanhsia is a backwoods town. It is certainly a conservative town, and one that has been spared (or deprived of, according to your orientation) the various drives toward change and expansion. There are a few small factories making fireworks and knitted sweaters, but most factory workers must ride a bus to jobs in other towns. The rice paddies come to the very edge of town on one side, and the tea plantations dominate the mountains on the other side. Most of the new houses are built to replace old ones, not to house new families. Sanhsia is not, however, a sleepy town. The shops seem to do a good business, the central market is lively with shoppers, peddlers, stall-owners, and farmers, and the streets are always crowded on festival days. Since Sanhsia is located on the edge of mountains that have excellent *hong-cui* (a mystical combination of land and waterways, which in this case ensures good burial sites), days that are deemed auspicious by the geomancers always bring two or three funeral processions through the town. The most elaborate are escorted by corps of motorcyclists, two or even three brass bands (playing such appropriate tunes as "Anchors Aweigh" and "Auld Lang Syne"), two or more traditional Taiwanese bands, and several flower-bedecked floats and banners. The bright blue and bright red gowns worn by some mourners and the colorfully decorated coffins make this display look less incongruous than it sounds to those who expect somber colors on somber occasions.

For the country people, Sanhsia is quite a satisfactory place. The variety of shops is sufficient to meet their material needs and numerous enough to provide entertainment on the days they come in to make purchases. The market is large enough to absorb their produce and yet small enough to allow them to maintain personal relationships with a number of stall-owners. To the people who live up in the mountains in lonely villages or isolated farmhouses, Sanhsia is a glittering urban center. Quite often an entire family, including the baby on his mother's back, will make a day's outing of a trip to town, concluding it with a visit to one of Sanhsia's two movie houses. There is often considerable restlessness toward the end of a film as the country people begin worrying about catching the last bus home. To miss it can mean a long hard walk after a full day or even tragedy, depending on how far away one's home is and how many relatives one has in Sanhsia.

In the pages that follow I am going to be concerned almost entirely with the attitudes and life styles of the country women who live in the Taipei basin. More specifically, I am going to describe the attitudes and behavior of the women I knew in Peihotien in 1958–60 and those I met in the area around Sanhsia in 1968. In 1958 Peihotien was a stable social unit in which all the members of the community were known to each other and in time to us.* The people I talked with in the countryside around Sanhsia were less well known to me, since I did not live among them and was there for only a few months. Until tea harvesting began to make my long walks into the edges of the mountains unprofitable (i.e., the women were all out picking tea, leaving only the dogs and the chickens at home), I concentrated on the families living

---

* Peihotien has been described more fully in my book *The House of Lim* (New York: Appleton-Century-Crofts, 1968).

up the narrow mountain valleys. In the late spring and early summer, when the heat and humidity made walking an ordeal, I spent more of my time talking to families living at the end of level paths in the paddy fields. None of my interviewing was far enough away from Sanhsia to produce a different orientation. All of the families faced Sanhsia, and all of them had lived for a long time in the location in which I found them. Although I found two or three families of newcomers, their women were the most suspicious and least cooperative of all the women I talked to. This in itself is a matter of ethnographic interest.

I have attempted in this chapter to place the culture of the Hokkien-speakers of Taiwan in its proper context as one variant of the many variants that make up Chinese culture. Although the evidence for the statements I make in the rest of the book about women and their lives is drawn solely from my husband's and my work in Taiwan, I believe that the general outlines of women's lives are much the same all over China. Unfortunately, information of this kind from other areas of China is at best sparse.

❧ 2 ❧

The Ongs of Peihotien

If you were to ask a few people in a country village on Taiwan who the members of their families are, you would probably come away with a sense of confusion. Men, women, the young, the middle-aged, and the elderly all have very different definitions of the family. Although this is a book about women, this chapter takes up the Chinese family, describing a particular Peihotien family from the customary point of view, i.e., with the focus on the men of the culture. Without this orientation it might be difficult for readers not familiar with the Chinese family to evaluate the quite different attitudes toward the family held by women.

Unlike the American family in which parents are expected to put the needs of their children above all else, the Chinese family places the weight of obligation on the child. For the gift of life, a boy is forever in his parents' debt. He owes them obedience, deference, and the most comfortable old age his income can provide, and after they die he must continue to provide for them in the spirit world. He is also obliged to see that another generation is born to carry on the duties to the ancestors after his own death. As we shall see in the pages that follow, Taiwanese farmers go to great trouble and expense to see that they have descendants. They tell the inquiring anthropologist that they must have sons to carry on their duties to the ancestors and to provide for their own support

14

in old age, but in more relaxed conversations they offer a subtler and perhaps more compelling reason. Most of the men we talked with were farmers of limited means whose dignity was mixed with resignation and who treated one another with the precise amount of respect each had earned. Yet each man felt he had a place in the world, and many of them could produce a written genealogy of one sort or another to show us the exact location of that place. His name, entered as the essential link between a carefully recorded, if mysterious, antiquity and the blank page of the future, gives him a quiet but unrefutable sense of value, of personal worth. The long list of men who preceded him is now dependent on him to carry on the family name and fortune. Few men would wish to be responsible for bringing such a history to a close.

In order to illustrate the various forms of marriage and adoption men employ to maintain the continuity of their line, I am going to take the reader on a tour of the history and present situation of a family we knew in Peihotien in 1958. The Ongs claim, citing their genealogy as evidence, to have been among the first settlers of Peihotien in the latter part of the eighteenth century. One of the Ongs, an elderly man with a great deal of family pride, told us that his family even predates the Lims, the predominate surname in the area. This is a traditional disagreement between Ongs and Lims, a matter not really worth our pursuit other than to note it as one of many examples of the barely concealed hostility between surname groups. At present the Ongs occupy two large houses, side by side, in a sea of Lims. Although on most days they would appear to be five separate families who happen to share sections of two adjoining farmhouses, on one particular day in May the men of all five families (or their female representatives) gather in the central hall of the older house to perform the ceremonies of respect for their most distant ancestor on the anniversary of his death. A few generations ago the forebears of these five families were one family, working the land and sharing its fruits as a unit, but the process of growth and division that typifies Chinese families has transformed them into several separate units who now share little more than their allegiance to a common line of ancestors. The Ongs living in the "new" house have not shared a stove (the colloquial expression for belonging to a joint living unit) with the Ongs in the old house since the middle of the last century. The three families that now occupy the old house shared a stove and a common purse until the end of World War II. Since we knew the "old-house Ongs" best, I will limit my description to them.

The grandfather of the present senior generation of Ongs died quite young, in his middle twenties, leaving two young sons. Although it is considered admirable in Chinese society for widows to remain faithful to their deceased husbands, never remarrying, this is an emotional luxury that peasant families cannot afford. A widow with two very young sons has little choice if she is to feed her children. In this case remarriage was imperative because the young father and his older brother had divided their property shortly after the birth of the younger brother's first son. After the younger man's death, the older brother was willing to guide and feed the small family for a while, but not indefinitely. Following a short period of mourning, his mother (the father was dead) began to look for a healthy young man to take over the responsibilities of the widow's family. A young widow sometimes returns to her own family, leaving her sons, who belong by law to the family of her husband. In this case, however, that course was not possible. The young widow had been adopted when she was eight months old and raised by her husband's parents. The adoption of girls was a common way of obtaining a bride for a son and a dutiful daughter-in-law for a family. Often these *sim-pua* (little daughters-in-law) did not know the whereabouts of their natal families, and even when they did, had a curious ambivalence about maintaining relations with them.

It is not easy to find a man who is willing to marry into a woman's family, even if the woman is a beautiful young virgin and the only child of a wealthy man. Although few men are required to change their surnames to that of their wives and to abandon their own ancestors, a man who has married into his wife's family is accused of doing just that. Even though he may have several older brothers who can carry on the sacrifices and provide descendants, he has still "abandoned his ancestors." It is assumed that any man willing to make this kind of marriage is flawed. It was several years before the family found someone to marry the young widow, and even then his terms were not really satisfactory to them. The man, named Tan, had been married before, but after ten years of childlessness his wife died, leaving him with an adopted son to raise. He had two older brothers, both of whom had more than enough children to keep their wives busy. Tan agreed to come and live as a son-in-law to the Ong family in order to have care for his son and rent-free land to work. He and his progeny could never inherit the land, which belonged to the two sons of the dead man. He refused to change his own surname to that of the Ongs, and he would not agree to give the Ong surname to any of the children he and the young widow might have. From the Ongs' point of view, these terms were bad, but Tan was the best they could find. The young widow may or may not have been consulted, but in discussing it the family now speaks as if it was not much of her business anyway.

Nevertheless, the marriage was satisfactory in some respects if not in others. Tan worked his stepsons' share of the Ong family land, taught all three boys the skills of agriculture, and provided them with a good stable life. Apparently he was sterile, for no more children were born, a circumstance that was tragic for him but probably a relief to the Ongs. The fact that his own son was an outsider in the Ong family became apparent when it was time for the young man to marry. Quite wealthy families adopted infants to raise as wives for their sons because they felt that incorporating a female from outside the family unit was less disruptive if it was accomplished when she was still a baby and could be raised to be a dutiful (and thoroughly browbeaten) daughter-in-law. For country people, a *sim-pua* marriage was also economically important. Bringing in an adult bride in the major patrilocal form of marriage could cost as much as a year's income, whereas the raising of a *sim-pua* cost no more than her food and clothing, and the wedding could be as simple as a bow to the ancestors and a slight change in the family's sleeping arrangements. For some reason the Ongs had not adopted *sim-pua* for their sons before the father's death. This is surprising, for 70 per cent of the Ongs' neighbors in Peihotien had chosen to raise wives for their sons. Perhaps the family was waiting for Mrs. Ong to bear a girl who could be given out in adoption and replaced at her mother's breast with a *sim-pua*. Girls who were old enough to be weaned were just that much more expensive and that much more difficult to incorporate. After young Ong's death, family circumstances were too straitened to consider adding another mouth or two to feed, and after Tan married in he may have had some reservations on just how many Ongs he was willing to provide for. Whatever the reasons, when the oldest Ong boy was in his early twenties he was married, at considerable expense, in the traditional manner. A few years later, when both the second Ong boy and the Tan boy were of an age to marry, the Ongs saw to it that the Ong boy was betrothed to a young woman from a respectable family, but more or less coerced Tan into "adopting" a twelve-year-old girl for his own son to marry "in a few years." This was probably all the Ongs were willing to spend on a boy who had no right to a share of the Ong property.

The Ongs are inclined to be somewhat vague about the events of the next few years, but according to the household registers, shortly after the marriage of his second stepson, Tan moved his wife and his two adopted children back to the district from which he had come. It may be that Tan felt his son would have better opportunities for work near his own family; it may be that part of the original agreement with the Ongs was that he would stay with them only until their grandsons were raised (not an uncommon arrangement in uxorilocal marriages); or it may be that the two Ong boys, now able to take care of their own land, decided (no doubt with strong backing from their Ong relatives) to ease the Tans out before they tried to lay claim to Ong land or capital. The present senior generation of Ongs (sons of the two Ong brothers) remember their grandmother as an old lady who came for long visits. They have little knowledge of their Tan relatives and in fact do not even invite them to their grand-mother's annual death day ceremonies.

The two Ong brothers were good farmers. They were also in the happy situation of owning all the land they could till and thus were not required, like most of their neighbors, to turn over large proportions of their harvest to landlords. Ong Cin-cai, who was four years older than Ong Cin-tik, served as family manager. Any cash surplus from the harvest he quickly loaned out to less fortunate farmers. Over the years the two brothers managed to add two small pieces of property to their estate and to replace their original house of mud and bamboo wattling with a large sturdy brick farmhouse, built wall by wall as their prosperity continued and topped eventually by a fine tile roof. At first the house was a simple rectangle partitioned into five rooms. In the center was a sizable guest hall

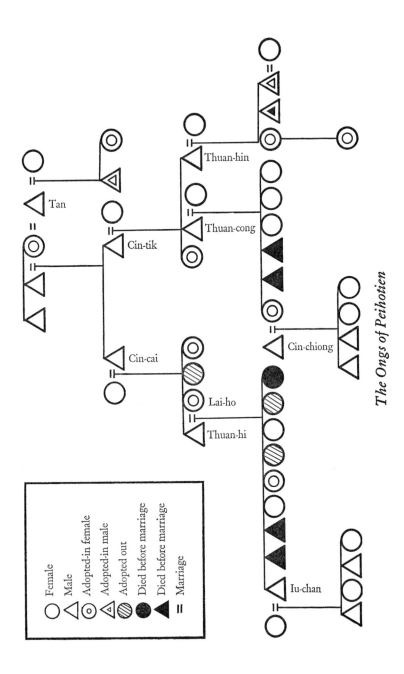

The Ongs of Peihotien

Legend:
- ○ Female
- △ Male
- ◎ Adopted-in female
- ◮ Adopted-in male
- ◍ Adopted out
- ● Died before marriage
- ◀ Died before marriage
- = Marriage

Tan
Cin-tik
Cin-cai
Thuan-hin
Thuan-cong
Cin-chiong
Lai-ho
Thuan-hi
Iu-chan

in which the Ongs' ancestral tablets were placed on an altar, facing the double-leaved doors. On either side of the central hall were sleeping rooms and storerooms, and in a lean-to at the back a substantial brick cooking stove. Cin-cai and his family occupied the rooms to the right (stage left) of the ancestral altar as was appropriate to his senior status, and Cin-tik, the younger brother, occupied the rooms on the other side. The contents of the bedrooms, much of which came in the dowries of the brothers' brides, were considered personal property, but the remainder of the house and its furnishings were the property of all. The two wives took turns preparing meals for the entire family.

Farmhouses in northern Taiwan are built to be easily enlarged. The ideal of every man is to see his sons and grandsons and even great-grandsons living in harmony under one roof, sharing their work and their wealth. Thus, in the original rectangle the Ong brothers put two doorways in the front in anticipation of the wings that would be added to house their numerous descendants. Today the wings are in place, and the structure is a complete U-shaped building. Unfortunately, the descendants have not been as numerous or as harmonious as the brothers might have hoped. It was three years before Cin-cai's wife finally bore him a live child, a boy. Two years later a girl was born. Cin-cai's mother was staying with them at the time, and she insisted that the girl be given away at once to one of the Tan family's neighbors. She also arranged for a baby girl she knew of in Tapu to be adopted as her first grandson's future wife. Although Cin-cai's wife objected (and according to the neighbors never really accepted the girl), the young man obeyed his mother and gave up his only daughter. This was the last child born to Cin-cai and his wife. Six years later, either because they wanted to "lead in a son" (i.e., encourage another pregnancy) or simply because they wanted a baby in the house, they adopted another girl.

Cin-tik's wife did not conceive immediately after marriage either, and once again the mother interfered. On one of her periodic visits she brought along a small girl just learning to walk and turned her over to Cin-tik's wife. It is a commonly held belief in Taiwan that the adoption of a girl will stimulate the birth of a son. Since many families are so anxious for descendants that they adopt a girl if the bride does not show signs of pregnancy within six months after marriage, the Taiwanese usually have innumerable examples of adopted daughters "leading in sons." Ong Cin-tik's wife, who eventually bore two sons, was no doubt considered an excellent example of the efficacy of the custom.

Ong Cin-cai and Ong Cin-tik continued to work their land jointly. Their sons were sent to the local school for a few years, and could both read and write. There was, of course, no need for the girls to acquire these skills. The boys also learned to farm, but it was apparent that five men could not be efficiently occupied by land that needed only two men. Cin-cai's son, Thuan-hi, found a job in a new winery that was built by the Japanese in Tapu. He was one of the first of the young men to find steady work outside the village that still allowed him to live at home. His parents were secretly proud of him and openly proud of themselves for having let him go to school. Cin-tik's eldest son, Thuan-cong, hated school, finding it nearly impossible to stay awake indoors. As soon as he finished his course at the primary school, he joined the older generation in the fields, earning some extra cash on feast days by working as a cook. He enjoyed cooking and over the years developed quite a talent for it. During our stay in Peihotien he was in great demand for the festivals that required large feasts. Cin-tik's younger son, Thuan-hin, excelled in school and would have liked to continue on to middle school, but that was considered too extravagant an ambition for a farmer's son. By virtue of his clear, not too elegant calligraphy, Thuan-hin got a job painting signs for the railroad. It was considered almost a white-collar job by his neighbors, and the Ongs were again quite pleased with their descendants.

Cin-cai's son and adopted daughter made their bow to the ancestors and were "pushed together," as the Taiwanese expression goes, shortly after the girl, Lai-ho, turned seventeen. Most young people loathed this form of marriage, finding sexual union with a person with whom they had been raised distasteful.* It was, in fact, one of the first customs rejected by the young once their potential economic independence gave them some power within the family. In 1914, however, Thuan-hi would have found it difficult to oppose his parents' demands on both economic and social grounds. In a Chinese marriage the goals of the family are primary, the interests of the individual secondary. For Thuan-hi to have refused to marry the young woman his parents had raised for that purpose would have been treachery. Although economically he was in a better position than those of his contemporaries who were dependent for a livelihood on land controlled by their fathers, it is unlikely that he earned enough at the winery to establish a separate household. By refusing to marry Lai-ho, he would have condemned himself to an existence on the fringe of his society, poor and disgraced, a prospect so unappealing that I rather doubt it did more than cross his mind, if that. For his sister-bride there were no alternatives—unless she was attractive enough to make her living as a prostitute. No doubt she simply submitted to the marriage as she had

* This subject is discussed in Chapter 10, but the reader who is interested in more information about incest and *sim-pua* marriages should consult Arthur P. Wolf's three articles on the subject: "Childhood Association, Sexual Attraction, and the Incest Taboo: A Chinese Case," *American Anthropologist*, 68, 4 (August 1966); "Adopt a Daughter-in-Law, Marry a Sister: A Chinese Solution to the Problem of the Incest Taboo," *ibid.*, 70, 5 (October 1968); and "Childhood Association and Sexual Attraction: A Further Test of the Westermarck Hypothesis," *ibid.*, 72, 3 (June 1970).

submitted to many other duties imposed on her by her lowly status in the family. Perhaps because the marriage was little more than another duty and not a very pleasant one, it was four years before she bore her husband a child. But in the end the family's goals were served. Along with several girls, Thuan-hi and his wife produced three sons. Two of them died as children, but one survived and through him the line was perpetuated.

Cin-tik's two sons experienced a great deal more difficulty in fulfilling their duties to the family. The elder, Thuan-cong, fathered three daughters and adopted another but produced no sons who lived to adulthood. The younger son, Thuan-hin, did not have any children at all. With daughters, Thuan-cong had the option of perpetuating his branch of the family by means of an uxorilocal marriage, and this is the choice he made. Thuan-hin could have followed his brother's example and made an uxorilocal marriage for his adopted daughter, but he chose to adopt a son. Male children are difficult to adopt, since few families are willing to part with precious descendants. A look at the number of children who died in the families of the relatively well-off Ongs indicates how realistic families were in wanting several sons to be sure that one lived to maturity. Ideally, a man without sons should adopt or name as his heir a brother's son or the grandson of his father's brother, but, as we have seen, the Ongs were very short of males in this generation. The alternative was to buy a male child from a stranger. Unfortunately, the child the Ongs bought was unhealthy, a risk one must take when one has dealings with "outsiders"—they cheat. The child died six months after he was adopted. It was some years before the family could afford another male adoption, and this time they approached it differently. One of the Ongs' neighbors had kept a mistress for several years in a nearby town. She died quite suddenly, leaving an adopted daughter and an infant son. Since the neighbor had three sons by his legal wife, he was not under any pressure to bring his illegitimate son home for his wife to raise—although he might respectably have done so. Instead he agreed to sell the child to Ong Thuan-hin and his wife. Thuan-hin's son is now a young man and is aware that he is adopted, but according to his foster mother he has no idea who his real parents are. I find this very unlikely in a village as small and gossipy as Peihotien. More probably this is a useful fiction for the young man as well as for his foster parents; no matter how intense (and praiseworthy) his filial feelings may be toward his natal parents, he can do nothing about expressing them since he does not know their identity.

The Chinese ideal of a man and his married brothers and all their married sons and grandsons pooling their resources and living in harmony under one roof is not commonly realized. Unusual circumstances or a fortunate combination of personalities may occur that will allow a large extended family to maintain a joint household for two or even three generations, but more often the friction between brothers or between their wives (or both) forces a division. Ong Cin-cai and Ong Cin-tik were among the few brothers who never divided their patrimony. Whether this was due to their amiability or, more important, that of their wives, I do not know. The present generation explains the stability of the family in economic terms. With three men working the land and two bringing in cash incomes the family thrived. If the land had been divided, either Cin-cai would have had to hire help or his son would have had to give up his outside job. Cin-tik, meanwhile, the father of two sons, would not have had quite enough land for even two adults to work profitably. Whatever the reasons, when Cin-tik died at the age of seventy-eight, the family was still united. It was united, but as with many families during World War II, it was disrupted.

To avoid Allied bombing raids, the Japanese moved the winery in which Ong Thuan-hi worked into the mountains. As a result, he was away from home for weeks at a time, returning home only for a day or two of rest before going back to the mountains. Thuan-hin was also away from home increasingly during this period as more and more work fell to the railroad men who were not called away into other areas of the war effort. Since Cin-cai and Cin-tik were too old to be of much use in the fields, the family land was left to the care of Thuan-hi's son and Thuan-cong. Although Cin-cai was still the head of the household, his son Thuan-hi had been making many of the decisions in his name. Now, with Thuan-hi's frequent absence, the responsibility fell on Thuan-cong as the senior responsible male. In 1942 Cin-tik died, and in the bleak months of confusion following the end of the war, Cin-cai followed him.

Thuan-hi remained at home for several months after his father's death, both because he had to supervise the funeral and because the winery was temporarily closed. He resumed headship of the family, making decisions now in his own rather than his father's name. In terms of Chinese succession, this was proper: he was the senior male of his generation. But in terms of the personalities involved and this particular situation, it was awkward. Thuan-cong had been making all the day-to-day decisions in the family for the last seven or eight years, allocating funds for purchases, vetoing those he considered unnecessary, representing the family in the community, and holding only token consultation with the absent Thuan-hi's son, Iu-chan. Thuan-hi's wife resented her husband's junior relative giving her orders, and she probably did little to soothe the resentment her son felt about his authority. She also saw to it that her daughter was provided with a particularly fine dowry, an extravagance that Thuan-cong remembers to this day with outrage. When Thuan-hi returned to his position at the head of the family, he found a group no longer united. Thuan-cong was unwilling to accept his supervision and asked almost at once that relatives be called in to supervise a formal division of the family.

By the time we arrived in Peihotien, Thuan-hi's half of the family was considerably reduced. His wife was dead, and all but the youngest of his daughters had been married or adopted out. He retired from the winery (which had moved back to Tapu) and was as restless as any American in the first months of retirement. He puttered about helping his son in the fields, but since much of their land had been sold, there really was not enough to keep him busy. Several years before, the family had opened a small general store (really almost a booth) in a nearby town. It has gradually become a fairly profitable enterprise. Thuan-hi's youngest daughter has run the store almost from the start, and in 1960 several members of the family were wondering about the fate of the store when the girl married. The girl herself was not eager to give up her interesting job for marriage, even though she was twenty-two and would soon pass the acceptable age for really "good" matches. If her mother had lived, the girl would probably have been married long before, but her brother's wife is unwilling to take the responsibility for arranging her marriage, and her father tends to brush away any inquiries the go-betweens make. Thuan-hi's eldest grandchild works as a salesman for a shirt manufacturer. His parents are criticized in the village for their laxness with him. He contributes a fair amount to the family budget, but his mother made the error of confiding to a relative that she has no idea how much he earns. He is, by village standards, extravagantly well dressed (with several pairs of shoes, we were told), but his mother defends this by saying that he is required to be smartly dressed in his job. She is probably quite right, though she will never convince her neighbors of it.

Following the family division, Cin-tik's two sons and their families lived together in their section of the farmhouse for nearly ten years. Both of the sons born to Thuan-cong died before they married, so when his adopted daughter was old enough to marry, he and his wife found a man willing to marry into their family and take their surname. Whenever anyone in Peihotien wishes to point to a successful uxorilocal marriage, they point to the Ongs. The young man in question was illegitimate by birth and was raised by anyone who would take him in. He is very considerate of his wife and more filial than many sons are to their parents.

Ong Thuan-hin has been quite fortunate in the two children he and his wife adopted. The elder, a girl, did so well in school that she was allowed to continue through middle school and subsequently found an excellent job in a bank. Over the years she has risen to a relatively high position for a woman. A few years ago, at the age of twenty-eight, she adopted a small girl. Such an adoption is common among prostitutes, who seek thereby to assure themselves of support in their old age, but it is a rather unusual step for a respectable young woman. Since banks will not trust married women to work with money, and Thuan-hin's daughter is too well paid to give up her job for an inferior uxorilocal marriage, she has chosen adoption as a means of satisfying her obligations to her parents. Thuan-hin's second adopted child, his son, is employed as a buyer for a distant relative's fluorescent light tube factory. His salary is not large, but as his family points out, at New Year he makes quite a bit in "gifts" from suppliers negotiating contracts.

According to the village gossips and by his own report, it was Ong Thuan-cong once again who was responsible for the division of this new family. Both halves of the family claim that there were no arguments at the time of the division, but in a minor disagreement just after division the latent hostility of the brothers came out in the open—to the point that they did not speak to each other for years. The following report by the wife of the younger brother, Thuan-hin, though clearly biased, gives some indication of the climate in a household about to divide.

When I first married into this family, I had to work very hard, and every morning I had to fix hand-warmers for [husband's] Older Brother's Wife and for [husband's] Mother. Every night I had to carry water for them to wash their feet. My husband's mother never had to tell me what to do. When I was cooking she never had to help me. But when Older Brother's Wife was cooking, she always went to help her. She always had to tell her what to do and when to do it. That's why Older Brother's Wife used to say our mother-in-law liked me best, but it wasn't true. She really liked her best. I just stayed out of trouble more. Before we divided the house my husband's older brother often used to bully me, so our home was not peaceful. When his wife's child was sick, he ran immediately for medicine, but when my child was sick and I asked for money to take him to get an injection, I never got it. I never had any money to spend on little things. Only my husband's mother used to feel sorry for me sometimes and give me a little.

It was [husband's] Older Brother who finally decided to invite the relatives to come and divide the family. When it came to dividing the house itself, the mediator said: "The people who live in the old part of the house can have the pig pens, the toilet, and the manure storage pit, plus four rooms. The one who takes the new part only has three rooms, so he also will get NT $2,000 from the one who takes the old part. Write old on one piece of paper and new on the other and choose that way." My husband's older brother said, "Oh, well, your son likes the new part best, so why don't you just take that." I was in the kitchen then and didn't hear this or I would have spoken up. My husband just agreed. My husband's older brother also asked for and got the water buffalo and even the better pieces of land. My husband just said, "All right. It's up to you." And that was the way it was divided. They got everything. We waited a long time before we got our money, too. That was because [husband's] Older Brother said we owed it to him. He said we built our kitchen on his land—and he wanted half the price of the whole plot for it—and we used some brick and tile left over from building the new part of the house to build our kitchen. Then he claimed he had paid for the doors on our house, and he wanted money for that too. I think what was really the matter was that he wanted to build a chicken house right on the back of our part of the house and I wouldn't let him. Think how it would smell in the summer! Anyway, we had to call the mediators back once, and when he started in about the kitchen I threatened to call them back again, so he finally stopped complaining about it.

But even then my husband and his brother were still speaking. It wasn't until the trouble over the water that his older brother stopped talking to him. After his paddy is filled, the water is turned into our land next. For some reason he decided to keep the water going into his fields longer than usual, and my husband had hired someone to come and plow in a few days, so he had to go and ask him to release the water. This made him mad.

Evidently, few words were exchanged in the fields, but as is so often the case with Chinese quarrels, that evening the older brother stood in his doorway and shouted his complaints against his younger brother for all the village to hear. The younger brother, a mild man, apparently did not respond publicly, but innumerable efforts by peacemakers failed to put the two back on speaking terms.

When we left Peihotien in 1961, there were both *the* Ong family, which gathered together on the death days of its shared ancestors to jointly present offerings, and five Ong families that cooked their evening meals on five separate stoves. When a man named Ong speaks of his family, he means the Ongs with whom he shares a stove (and that may include his brother and his brother's children) and he means a larger group, the Ongs long dead and the Ongs yet unborn. In some areas of China—in fact just a few miles from where this particular Ong family lives — there still exist real lineages, corporate groups that own land in common and maintain an ancestral hall to house their ancestral tablets. But for the men of Peihotien, the larger family seemed to include only their direct lineal ascendants (fathers, grandfathers, etc.) and their own descendants. It is obvious from the preceding pages that a man's attitude toward events in his household is greatly influenced by his obligations to his larger family. To satisfy the needs of his ancestors for descendants (and his own need to be respectable in a culture that demands he satisfy the needs of his ancestors), a man will marry his sister, force his daughter to marry a man she loathes, and sell his granddaughter. Customary law in China leaves women nearly powerless to control their own fates. Nevertheless, without at least the partial cooperation of the women the most deeply rooted values of their menfolk cannot be maintained. In the next chapter we will examine the quite different view women have of the family, and the way they have come to manipulate its needs to provide for their own.

※ 3 ※

Uterine Families
and the Women's Community

Few women in China experience the continuity that is typical of the lives of the menfolk. A woman can and, if she is ever to have any economic security, must provide the links in the male chain of descent, but she will never appear in anyone's genealogy as that all-important name connecting the past to the future. If she dies before she is married, her tablet will not appear on her father's altar; although she was a temporary member of his household, she was not a member of his family. A man is born into his family and remains a member of it throughout his life and even after his death. He is identified with the family from birth, and every action concerning him, up to and including his death, is in the context of that group. Whatever other uncertainties may trouble his life, his place in the line of ancestors provides a permanent setting. There is no such secure setting for a woman. She will abruptly leave the household into which she is born, either as an infant or as an adult bride, and enter another whose members treat her with suspicion or even hostility.

A man defines his family as a large group that includes the dead, the not-yet-born, and the living members of his household. But how does a woman define her family? This is not a question that China specialists often consider, but from their treatment of the family in general, it would seem that a woman's family is identical with that of the senior male in the household in which she lives. Although I have never asked, I imagine a Taiwanese man would define a woman's family in very much those same terms. Women, I think, would give quite a different answer. They do not have an unchanging place, assigned at birth, in any group, and their view of the family reflects this.

When she is a child, a woman's family is defined for her by her mother and to some extent by her grandmother. No matter how fond of his daughter the father may be, she is only a temporary member of his household and useless to his family—he cannot even marry her to one of his sons as he could an adopted daughter. Her irrelevance to her father's family in turn affects the daughter's attitude toward it. It is of no particular interest to her, and the need to maintain its continuity has little meaning for her beyond the fact that this continuity matters a great deal to some of the people she loves. As a child she probably accepts to some degree her grandmother's orientation toward the family: the household, i.e., those people who live together and eat together, including perhaps one or more of her father's married brothers and their children. But the group that has the most meaning for her and with which she will have the most lasting ties is the smaller, more cohesive unit centering on her mother, i.e., the uterine family—her mother and her mother's children. Father is important to the group, just as grandmother is important to some of the children, but he is not quite a member of it, and for some uterine families he may even be "the enemy." As the girl grows up and her grandmother dies and a brother or two marries, she discovers that her mother's definition of the family is becoming less exclusive and may even include such outsiders as her brother's new wife. Without knowing precisely when it happened, she finds that her brother's interests and goals have shifted in a direction she cannot follow. Her mother does not push her aside, but when the mother speaks of the future, she

33

speaks in terms of her son's future. Although the mother sees her uterine family as adding new members and another generation, her daughter sees it as dissolving, leaving her with strong particular relationships, but with no group to which she has permanent loyalties and obligations.

When a young woman marries, her formal ties with the household of her father are severed. In one of the rituals of the wedding ceremony the bride's father or brothers symbolically inform her by means of spilt water that she, like the water, may never return, and when her wedding sedan chair passes over the threshold of her father's house, the doors are slammed shut behind her. If she is ill-treated by her husband's family, her father's family may intervene, but unless her parents are willing to bring her home and support her for the rest of her life (and most parents are not), there is little they can do beyond shaming the other family. This is usually enough.

As long as her mother is alive, the daughter will continue her contacts with her father's household by as many visits as her new situation allows. If she lives nearby she may visit every few days, and no matter where she lives she must at least be allowed to return at New Year. After her mother dies her visits may become perfunctory, but her relations with at least one member of her uterine family, the group that centered on her mother, remain strong. Her brother plays an important ritual role throughout her life. She may gradually lose contact with her sisters as she and they become more involved with their own children, but her relations with her brother continue. When her sons marry, he is the guest of honor at the wedding feasts, and when her daughters marry he must give a small banquet in their honor. If her sons wish to divide their father's estate, it is their mother's brother who is called on to supervise. And when she dies, the coffin cannot be closed until her brother determines to his own satisfaction that she died a natural death and that her husband's family did everything possible to prevent it.

With the ritual slam of her father's door on her wedding day, a young woman finds herself quite literally without a family. She enters the household of her husband—a man who in an earlier time, say fifty years ago, she would never have met and who even today, in modern rural Taiwan, she is unlikely to know very well. She is an outsider, and for Chinese an outsider is always an object of deep suspicion. Her husband and her father-in-law do not see her as a member of their family. But they do see her as essential to it; they have gone to great expense to bring her into their household for the purpose of bearing a new generation for their family. Her mother-in-law, who was mainly responsible for negotiating the terms of her entry, may harbor some resentment over the hard bargaining, but she is nonetheless eager to see another generation added to *her* uterine family. A mother-in-law often has the same kind of ambivalence toward her daughter-in-law as she has toward her husband—the younger woman seems a member of her family at times and merely a member of the household at others. The new bride may find that her husband's sister is hostile or at best condescending, both attitudes reflecting the daughter's distress at an outsider who seems to be making her way right into the heart of the family.

Chinese children are taught by proverb, by example, and by experience that the family is the source of their security, and relatives the only people who can be depended on. Ostracism from the family is one of the harshest sanctions that can be imposed on erring youth. One of the reasons mainlanders as individuals are considered so untrustworthy on Taiwan is the fact that they are not subject to the controls of (and therefore have no fear of ostracism from) their families. If a timid new bride is considered an object of suspicion and potentially dangerous because she is a stranger, think how uneasy her own

35

first few months must be surrounded by strangers. Her irrelevance to her father's family may result in her having little reverence for descent lines, but she has warm memories of the security of the family her mother created. If she is ever to return to this certainty and sense of belonging, a woman must create her own uterine family by bearing children, a goal that happily corresponds to the goals of the family into which she has married. She may gradually create a tolerable niche for herself in the household of her mother-in-law, but her family will not be formed until she herself forms it of her own children and grandchildren. In most cases, by the time she adds grandchildren, the uterine family and the household will almost completely overlap, and there will be another daughter-in-law struggling with loneliness and beginning a new uterine family.

The ambiguity of a man's position in relation to the uterine families accounts for much of the hostility between mother-in-law and daughter-in-law. There is no question in the mind of the older woman but that her son *is* her family. The daughter-in-law might be content with this situation once her sons are old enough to represent her interests in the household and in areas strictly under men's control, but until then, she is dependent on her husband. If she were to be completely absorbed into her mother-in-law's family—a rare occurrence unless she is a *sim-pua*—there would be little or no conflict; but under most circumstances she must rely on her husband, her mother-in-law's son, as her spokesman, and here is where the trouble begins. Since it is usually events within the household that she wishes to affect, and the household more or less overlaps with her mother-in-law's uterine family, even a minor foray by the younger woman suggests to the older one an all-out attack on everything she has worked so hard to build in the years of her own loneliness and insecurity. The birth of grandchildren further complicates their relations, for the one sees them as new members for her family and the other as desperately needed recruits to her own small circle of security.

In summary, my thesis contends (and the material found in the rest of the book will show what led me to it) that because we have heretofore focused on men when examining the Chinese family—a reasonable approach to a patrilineal system— we have missed not only some of the system's subtleties but also its near-fatal weaknesses. With a male focus we see the Chinese family as a line of descent, bulging to encompass all the members of a man's household and spreading out through his descendants. With a female focus, however, we see the Chinese family not as a continuous line stretching between the vague horizons of past and future, but as a contemporary group that comes into existence out of one woman's need and is held together insofar as she has the strength to do so, or, for that matter, the need to do so. After her death the uterine family survives only in the mind of her son and is symbolized by the special attention he gives her earthly remains and her ancestral tablet. The rites themselves are demanded by the ideology of the patriliny, but the meaning they hold for most sons is formed in the uterine family. The uterine family has no ideology, no formal structure, and no public existence. It is built out of sentiments and loyalties that die with its members, but it is no less real for all that. The descent lines of men are born and nourished in the uterine families of women, and it is here that a male ideology that excludes women makes its accommodations with reality.

Women in rural Taiwan do not live their lives in the walled courtyards of their husband's households. If they did, they might be as powerless as their stereotype. It is in their relations in the outside world (and for women in rural Taiwan that world consists almost entirely of the village) that women develop sufficient backing to maintain some independence under their powerful mothers-in-law and even occasionally to bring the men's world to terms. A successful venture into the men's world is no small feat when one recalls that the men of a village were born there and are often related to one another, whereas the women are unlikely to have either the ties of childhood or the ties of kinship to unite them. All the same, the needs, shared interests, and common problems of women are reflected in every village in a loosely knit society that can when needed be called on to exercise considerable influence.

Women carry on as many of their activities as possible outside the house. They wash clothes on the riverbank, clean and pare vegetables at a communal pump, mend under a tree that is a known meetingplace, and stop to rest on a bench or group of stones with other women. There is a continual moving back and forth between kitchens, and conversations are carried on from open doorways through the long, hot afternoons of summer. The shy young girl who enters the village as a bride is examined as frankly and suspiciously by the women as an animal that is up for sale. If she is deferential to her elders, does not criticize or compare her new world unfavorably with the one she has left, the older residents will gradually accept her presence on the edge of their conversations and stop changing the topic to general subjects when she brings the family laundry to scrub on the rocks near them. As the young bride meets other girls in her position, she makes allies for the future, but she must also develop relationships with the older women. She learns to use considerable discretion in making and receiving confidences, for a girl who gossips freely about the affairs of her husband's household may find herself labeled a troublemaker. On the other hand, a girl who is too reticent may find herself always on the outside of the group, or worse yet, accused of snobbery. I described in *The House of Lim* the plight of Lim Chui-ieng, who had little village backing in her troubles with her husband and his family as the result of her arrogance toward the women's community. In Peihotien the young wife of the storekeeper's son suffered a similar lack of support. Warned by her husband's parents not to be too "easy" with the other villagers lest they try to buy things on credit, she obeyed to the point of being considered unfriendly by the women of the village. When she began to have serious troubles with her husband and eventually his family, there was no one in the village she could turn to for solace, advice, and most important, peacemaking.

Once a young bride has established herself as a member of the women's community, she has also established for herself a certain amount of protection. If the members of her husband's family step beyond the limits of propriety in their treatment of her—such as refusing to allow her to return to her natal home for her brother's wedding or beating her without serious justification—she can complain to a woman friend, preferably older, while they are washing vegetables at the communal pump. The story will quickly spread to the other women, and one of them will take it on herself to check the facts with another member of the girl's household. For a few days the matter will be thoroughly discussed whenever a few women gather. In a young wife's first few years in the community, she can expect to have her mother-in-law's side of any disagreement given fuller weight than her own—her mother-in-law has, after all, been a part of the community a lot longer. However, the discussion itself will serve to curb many offenses. Even if the older woman knows that public opinion is falling to her side, she will still be somewhat more judicious about refusing her daughter-in-law's next request. Still, the daughter-in-law who hopes to make use of the village forum to depose her mother-in-law or at least gain herself special privilege will discover just how important the prerogatives of age and length of residence are. Although the women can serve as a powerful protective force for their defenseless younger members, they are also a very conservative force in the village.

Taiwanese women can and do make use of their collective power to lose face for their menfolk in order to influence decisions that are ostensibly not theirs to make. Although young women may have little or no influence over their husbands and would not dare express an unsolicited opinion (and perhaps not even a solicited one) to their fathers-in-law, older women who have raised their sons properly retain considerable influence over their sons' actions, even in activities exclusive to men. Further, older women who have displayed years of good judgment are regularly consulted by their husbands about major as well as minor economic and social projects. But even men who think themselves free to ignore the opinions of their women are never free of their own concept, face. It is much easier to lose face than to have face. We once asked a male friend in Peihotien just what "having face" amounted to. He replied, "When no one is talking about a family, you can say it has face." This is precisely where women wield their power. When a man behaves in a way that they consider wrong, they talk about him—not only among themselves, but to their sons and husbands. No one "tells him how to mind his own business," but it becomes abundantly clear that he is losing face and by continuing in this manner may bring shame to the family of his ancestors and descendants. Few men will risk that.

The rules that a Taiwanese man must learn and obey to be a successful member of his society are well developed, clear, and relatively easy to stay within. A Taiwanese woman must also learn the rules, but if she is to be a successful woman, she must learn not to stay within them, but to *appear* to stay within them; to manipulate them, but not to appear to be manipulating them; to teach them to her children, but not to depend on her children for her protection. A truly successful Taiwanese woman is a rugged individualist who has learned to depend largely on herself while appearing to lean on her father, her husband, and her son. The contrast between the terrified young bride and the loud, confident, often lewd old woman who has outlived her mother-in-law and her husband reflects the tests met and passed by not strictly following the rules and by making purposeful use of those who must. The Chinese male's conception of women as "narrow-hearted" and socially inept may well be his vague recognition of this facet of women's power and technique.

The women's subculture in rural Taiwan is, I believe, below the level of consciousness. Mothers do not tell their about-to-be married daughters how to establish themselves in village society so that they may have some protection from an oppressive family situation, nor do they warn them to gather their children into an exclusive circle under their own control. But girls grow up in village society and see their mothers and sisters-in-law settling their differences to keep them from a public airing or presenting them for the women's community to judge. Their mothers have created around them the meaningful unit in their fathers' households, and when they are desperately lonely and unhappy in the households of their husbands, what they long for is what they have lost. I will have several occasions in the following pages to point out areas in the subculture of women that mesh perfectly into the main culture of the society. The two cultures are not symbiotic because they are not sufficiently independent of one another, but neither do they share identical goals or necessarily use the same means to reach the goals they do share. Outside the village the women's subculture seems not to exist. The uterine family also has no public existence, and appears almost as a response to the traditional family organized in terms of a male ideology.

4

Friends and Neighbors

In the chapters that follow I will be examining the life cycles of women and their relations with both their husband's family and their uterine family, but first we must look at the setting within which women in rural Taiwan come to terms with their families. Because I believe concrete examples are more convincing than abstract models, this chapter is devoted to a tour of the women's community in one small village, the one I knew best, Peihotien. In the late 1950's there were thirty-six houses in Peihotien, but there were nearly twice as many families. Several of the larger farmhouses held four and five families of the same surname, the result of the kind of family divisions I described in Chapter 2. In some cases the heads of the various households were sons or grandsons of the same man; in other cases, the divisions were even further back in their genealogies. Although labeled in the same way as the other houses on the accompanying map of the village, these units are more properly called compounds. Often when a family divided or became too large for its house, it either added a wing or built an adjoining structure. As a result there was a tendency for male kin to be close neighbors. Spatially, Peihotien is a small place, and if the kin ties of men had been the defining factor in the friendships of their wives and daughters-in-law, it would not have been difficult for a woman to walk just a few doors one way rather than the other to join the wives of her husband's kinsmen for an afternoon visit. Instead, women gathered around a shared working place, a convenient visiting area, or an attractive personality. The men who lived in House 38 were closely related to the men who lived a few hundred yards away in House 16, but the women from these households spent their leisure and working hours with a different set of women, in general their closer neighbors.

We had not lived in Peihotien long before we could identify the five neighborhood groups that compose the women's community. These were the women who were likely to be found washing clothes together, minding one another's babies, or simply chatting together. Each group included women of all ages, ranging from the youngest bride to an aged great-grandmother. An unmarried daughter, if she was a member of any group, belonged to her mother's group; a daughter-in-law was nearly always a member of her mother-in-law's group. Each group usually had at its core a handful of middle-aged women who had long been resident in Peihotien. They were, informally, its leaders, the women to whom younger women turned for advice and help when life in their husband's household seemed unendurable. They knew everything and were in a real sense the anthropologist's best friend or worst enemy, for they could open as many doors for him as they could close. Fortunately, they found our young female field assistant as charming as we did and seemed happy to answer her less-than-innocent questions in exchange for the detailed information she could provide about us as a member of our household.

The Alley, our name for the only path into the village large enough to accommodate an automobile, was the center for one of the neighborhood groups. The two sisters-in-law who lived in House 10 were unusual in that they were genuinely fond of each other and of each other's children. Their open, friendly personalities encouraged their neighbors to drop in

43

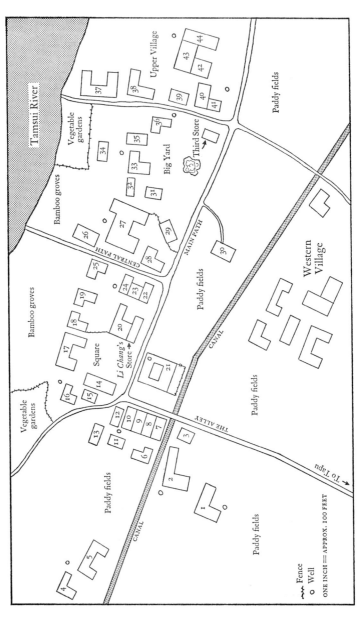

The Village of Peihotien

for a moment's chat whenever they wished, and we rarely went to their house without finding at least one neighbor discussing the events of the day. The women from Houses 6, 7, 8, and 9 put their heads in the door a dozen times a day on their way to the nearby well, or to the store, or to look for a missing child. None of the husbands of these women were related to one another, although several of them had kinsmen elsewhere in Peihotien. Relations between the women in the compound marked House 2 were strained, and had been for several years as the result of a particularly acrimonious family division. They were all, nonetheless, active members of the Alley Group, and I had the impression that they interacted with one another more in House 10 and other Alley homes than in their own shared courtyard. To our surprise, even the wife of the mainlander living in House 3 visited in House 10, and when she had a baby, the kindly sisters-in-law there organized the neighbors to care for her other children and cook for her. The fifteen women in Houses 4 and 5 were all married to the descendants of the eldest man's grandfather. Their houses were some distance from the other houses in Peihotien, but even though they had their own well, a good path to the river, and a washing platform on the irrigation canal that passed their front doors, they often carried up a few articles of clothing to join the other women of the Alley Group at the platform on the canal next to House 3. This washing platform, nothing more than a few feet of smooth concrete in the irrigation canal, was a favorite gathering place for women in the Alley Group. It was coolly shaded by a tree and buildings and commanded an excellent view of anyone entering or leaving the village on the way to Tapu. The two women in House 1 worked with their husbands selling fish in Tapu and had little free time to visit with their neighbors, but if the fish were sold out early, they often came here in the late afternoon to do their laundry or wash out their baskets, forsaking the more convenient water supply in their own compound. Their father-in-law was a close kinsman of the men in House 2, but the women, though friendly, seemed no closer to their womenfolk than to the other Alley women. The women in Houses 11, 12, and 13 also had a well near their homes, but they preferred to use the social canal platform.

A second neighborhood group used the benches in front of the *Li Chang*'s Store as its focal point. The store sold most of the daily necessities (excluding meat and vegetables) at prices only slightly higher than in Tapu. The woman who ran the store was the wife of a former *Li Chang*, hence the name.* She was a quiet, shy woman whose closest friend was her husband's older brother's daughter-in-law, a woman half her age. Both women were members of the neighborhood group, but neither was a leader. Perhaps it was simply the older woman's friendly shyness that made the benches at the store an easy place for other women to gather, exchange gossip, and evaluate the behavior of passersby. The family in House 14 also sold small items like cigarettes and candy from a window in the front room, but the house had not become a gathering place for other women. All the women living on the Square, including the women from House 14, dropped by the *Li Chang*'s Store several times a day to chat, to ask if anyone knew where their child (or friend) was, and occasionally to buy. The men in Houses 18, 19, and 20 were closely related, descendants of the same grandfather, but the women from these families, particularly those in Houses 18 and 19, were notorious for their quarrels, which usually grew out of a squabble among their children. Unlike the women from House 2, who seemed to use their neighborhood group as a way of gradually returning to friendly relations, these women *needed* their neighborhood group to act as mediators. One of

* A *Li Chang* is something like a mayor and is responsible for a very small district.

the women whose opinion carried great weight in the *Li Chang*'s Store Group was Lim A-pou, a woman in her late forties who was adopted into House 21 as an infant. She worked very hard and had little time to spare for idle gossip, but one frequently heard the query, "What does A-pou think about it?" The women from Houses 23, 24, and 25 were also members of the *Li Chang*'s Store Group.

Among the related families living in the big compound labeled House 27, there were eleven adult women. Some of them were close friends; others were merely friendly toward each other. All of these women were more likely to wash clothes together, market for one another, and gossip together than to interact with women outside their compound. Although we sometimes met one of the House 27 women in other village homes, we rarely found women from outside their compound visiting them. This seemed to be one of the few groups of women whose social relations were strongly influenced by the kinship of their husbands, yet even here the kin ties of the men were apparently offset by the confines of geography. The men in House 27 worshiped the same ancestors as the men in Houses 41 and 42 in Upper Village, but there was almost no contact between the women in these families. By virtue of a fortunate combination of personalities, the women in House 27 had become an overlap of male kinship group and a neighborhood group, and the result was the only really solidary group of women in the village. When Lim Ciou-ti, an elderly member of the House 27 Group, became involved in a dispute with a woman from another neighborhood over a quarrel between Ciou-ti's precious grandson and the other woman's son, a quarrel that later escalated into whispers of sorcery, Ciou-ti and her housemates were criticized as a group and responded as a group.

In the Big Yard there was a huge old tree shading a cluster of big stones that provided a natural gathering place for another neighborhood. Most of the women in the Big Yard Group were drawn from the houses that form the natural boundaries of the open area, with two exceptions. In terms of sheer geography, I would have expected the women in House 28 to interact largely with the women in House 27, but we found them most often with the women from the Big Yard Group. A more telling example is that of the woman who lived in House 26 and drew water from the same well as the House 27 Group. She and her husband and children had moved to Peihotien nearly ten years before we came, and she told us that it had been a lonely ten years. Her children went to school and played with the children from House 27, but she held the gossip and unfriendliness of their mothers responsible for the slowness with which she had been accepted into the community. She visited with women from the Big Yard Group and from the *Li Chang*'s Store Group, but she was not really a member of either. Her bitterness toward the cliquish behavior of the House 27 Group may be well founded, but her isolation was not entirely their doing. Most outsiders make their way into the women's community under the sponsorship of a guarantor, their mother-in-law. We watched with pity the struggles of a lively young bride, who came with only her husband to live in Peihotien, as she tried to make a place for herself in the women's community. The rooms she and her husband were renting belonged to a distant but traceable relative (the husband's parents were dead), and both she and her husband had been school friends of the children of another village family. However, neither the relatives nor the friends were willing to present her to the community as their responsibility. All the women gossiped about her social blunders, but none was willing to explain to her the intricacies of village etiquette. She wandered from group to group and conversation to conversation, losing more ground each time she tried to contribute her anecdote or bit of scandal. When we left Peihotien, she was still, after a year, a familiar outsider.

The women who lived in Upper Village (so named because they lived upstream and the river was once the orienting dimension in Peihotien) formed another neighborhood group. Of the fifteen families who lived there, ten bore the surname Lim, but two of the Lim families who lived in House 38 could not tell us how they were related to the other Lims in Upper Village, and the Lims in House 43 were more closely related to a branch of the Lims in a nearby village. The women from the eight families in Houses 37 and 38 (Lims, Tans, and Ongs) shared a well and a drying ground and thus saw more of each other than they did of their friends and relatives in Houses 39–44, but there was a great deal of visiting back and forth through the back doors and as the women from Houses 39–44 moved to and from the river. The Third Store, which was run by a woman from House 37, drew women from both complexes to sit and talk on the bench she provided. Gim-siu had established her little store, selling candy, cookies, cigarettes, and similar small items, on the corner of the paths in hopes of attracting customers from Western Village as well. In that regard she has not been very successful. Although many of the men in Peihotien and Western Village had close kinship ties and participated in the same religious cycles and agricultural associations, we rarely found children from Western Village in the play groups in Peihotien, and if their mothers came to the Third Store to make purchases, they did not stop to gossip. We occasionally met Western Village women in Peihotien—indeed, several of them had sisters and daughters living there—but they came as outsiders.

Now, the neighborhood groups having been identified, they must be blended back into their natural settings in the women's community, for though every woman was aware of them, they were not in any sense cliques or factions within the community. Some women, particularly older women whose daughters-in-law had relieved them of many household chores, were involved in the affairs of more than one neighborhood. Most women had at least one close friend or kinswoman in a neighborhood group other than her own. Although the kinship of their menfolk did not dictate the friendship of the women, it did serve to provide newcomers, i.e., brides, with a wider circle of acquaintances. For a few women these early, rather formal relationships matured into real friendships. The friendships of women who grew up in Peihotien were often those formed in childhood. Siu-khim, a middle-aged member of the Upper Village Group, was adopted as a child into an Ong family and later married her foster brother. Lim A-pou of the *Li Chang*'s Store Group entered the village at about the same time under similar circumstances. She was married to her foster brother in a Lim family. As adults they remained close friends and were frequently to be found visiting with each other and with each other's neighborhood group.

Two stores in the village, the *Li Chang*'s Store and the Third Store, also served to erase the lines between neighborhood groups. Women from all the neighborhoods were dependent on the *Li Chang*'s Store for items forgotten on their last trip to the market town, and for candy to quiet a demanding child. Before Gim-siu opened the Third Store, her daily contacts were more likely to be with her neighbors in Upper Village, but as a storekeeper on the path between the Big Yard and Upper Village she was as well informed about the goings on in one group as in the other.

There were also women who had kin ties of their own in the village. The adoptive sister of a woman who married into House 38 married into a family at the opposite end of the village, House 5. They frequently brought their children to play together while the mothers cooperated in making pickles or sewing the covers on clumsy bedding. Another woman, Lim So-lan, grew up as an adopted daughter in House 27, and she was one of the few village women who regularly visited there. Besides her membership in the Alley Group and her frequent visits in House 27, gentle Lim So-lan also considered Tan Bi-ni, a loud-voiced woman in the Big Yard Group, her dearest friend. Yet another web of friendships that cross-cut four neighborhood groups centered on Ong A-ti. Until shortly before we entered the village Ong A-ti, a woman in her late fifties, lived in House 15 and was very much a part of the *Li Chang*'s Store Group, although she had two very close friends in other neighborhoods, one a woman from House 2 and the other from the opposite end of the village in House 44. After her family built a new house in the middle of the paddy that separated Peihotien from Western Village (House 30), she was still to be found frequently at the *Li Chang*'s Store, but since the path to her new house entered the Main Path near the shade tree in the Big Yard, she often came out to chat with that group.

At every river the traveler in Taiwan will notice anywhere from a handful to a villageful of women squatting on its banks washing clothes. Peihotien was blessed with some particularly fine flat rocks on the banks of the Tamsui, just at the foot of the Central Path. At any hour of the day, rain or shine, there were likely to be women there doing their laundry, making it last as long as the conversation or the company was amusing. Early in our stay in Peihotien we learned, as did the brides in the village, that the most congenial way to study the social life of the women's community was to join the women on the rocks. Sooner or later nearly every woman in the village, including the women from House 27, came to the river to wash and to talk.

The neighborhood groups in Peihotien could easily have been a divisive factor in the women's community, but they were not. The groups were casual, had overlapping membership, and were veined with ties that crossed and combined them. The only incident we observed during our long stay in Peihotien in which the women of a neighborhood seemed to take sides on an issue as members of a group was the quarrel involving House 27. That incident is worth noting because it may indicate just how divisive the effect of male kin ties might have been if they had in fact defined all the friendship ties of women. This was not by any means the only dispute between women that we witnessed in Peihotien, but in every other case those who lined up behind the principals did so over the issue, and were as likely to be from one neighborhood as from another. The final peacemakers represented the community of women, not one of its neighborhoods. The neighborhood groups were important to the quality of women's everyday existence in Peihotien, but their other ties prevented exclusive groups from forming. It was perhaps from this weakness that the women's community gained its strength. The women were too dependent on the delicate mesh of friendship to allow it to become divisive.

⚜ 5 ⚜

Little Girls

The only proper place for a Taiwanese child to enter the world is in its father's paternal home. In 1958 only two Peihotien women had given birth in a hospital; in Sanhsia in 1968 hospital births were fairly frequent among the townsfolk, but the country people still considered hospitals an extravagance and not really in the best interests of the children. Even the country people who could afford hospitals felt that a child born there was not given the best start in life. At home a newborn child is given honey and water or mild ginseng tea until his mother's milk comes in—a treatment that comforts the infant and is believed to prevent several skin diseases —but the hospitals will not allow such supplemental feedings.

One of the goals of my husband's first field trip to Taiwan in 1957 was to carry out a study of Chinese child-training practices. The study was modeled after Whiting, Lambert, and Child's "Six Culture Project." We selected a sample of sixty-four children, thirty-two boys and thirty-two girls, in the village of Peihotien and interviewed them (insofar as one can interview children between the ages of four and seven) and their parents. We carried out a rigorous schedule of carefully timed observations of each child in a number of settings and made a more informal series of observations of their forty-odd mothers and families. My husband, Arthur Wolf, has kindly allowed me to skim the cream off his data in the next two chapters on children. Since he will present a more systematic analysis of this material elsewhere, I will not include here tables or tests of significance. For a detailed description of the interviews and methodology, I refer the reader to J. W. M. Whiting, Irvin L. Child, William W. Lambert, et al., *Field Guide for the Study of Socialization* (New York: John Wiley, 1966).

53

Homes of friends or relatives, even the mother-to-be's parents, are considered quite out of the question as a site for childbirth, not because of any danger to the mother or child, but because of the high cost to the hosts. As a Chinese proverb puts it: "It is better to loan your house for a death than for a birth." This proverb reflects the widely held belief that a family's fortune holds only a certain number of descendants. If an outsider is allowed to bear a child in the family's home, the family is allowing one of its descendants to be born to someone else.

Beyond the expense and danger of a hospital and the ritual impropriety of bearing a child in someone else's home, it is simply considered proper for a son, and all unborn children are presumed to be sons, to be born in the home of his ancestors. Like many agriculturalists, the Chinese have a strong attachment to place, and if things are to be done properly, be they births, weddings, or funerals, the present generation should do them in the same place as the ancestors before them and the descendants after them. For the Taiwanese, "home" acquires at least part of its significance from the fact that it symbolizes the kinship group and a line of descent. In one of the farm families I met in 1968, a college-educated son brought his wife "home" to give birth to their first child, exchanging their urban apartment and big city medical facilities for a clean but drafty farmhouse, an ill-trained if very experienced midwife, and a mother-in-law.

In the "old days," the most crucial decision in a female's life was made in the few moments after she was born. If the family had a surfeit of girls, she was simply allowed to slip into a bucket of water, and that was the end of it. If, however, she was the mother's first child or at least her first girl, or if the family felt it might be useful to exchange the new infant for another girl baby who could later be married to a son, she was allowed to live. Today all children are allowed to live. A newborn girl may not be greeted with the same rejoicing that is her brother's portion, but she receives basically the same treatment. The midwife bathes her, ties her hands loosely so that she will be obedient and not meddlesome, and instructs the family to prepare either its own or the midwife's favorite concoction to "reduce the heat" (which causes babies to have red faces at birth) and to nurture the child until the mother has milk. The midwife returns in three days to bathe the baby again and claim her payment, which is a little less when she officiates at the birth of a female child.

On the third day after the child's birth—when there is more certainty that it will live—offerings of rice and peanuts are made to Chng Bu, the Bed Mother. She is asked to provide her protection and help in raising this child and the children to follow. From the birth of the first child until the pubescence of the lastborn child, or stated differently, as long as there is a child in the house, Chng Bu is among the collection of gods and ancestors that receive offerings on the first and fifteenth of each lunar month as well as on any major festivals. Every person I asked assured me that Chng Bu could not help in promoting fertility; nonetheless three days after a wedding every mother-in-law offers the little god a sacrifice of oily rice decorated with a flower famous for its productivity. The offering may of course be simply anticipatory.

Shortly after the first child's birth, whether it be a boy or a girl, the maternal grandparents are informed of the event by a gift of oily rice, wine, and chicken. The births of all subsequent sons are announced in this way, but the birth of a daughter to a family that already has children calls for simpler gifts, e.g., the oily rice alone. The new mother's parents are expected to send her a personal gift as well as six chickens, wine, and a special kind of noodles. To a firstborn son and, if they can afford it, to later-born sons, the maternal grandparents send a year's supply of clothing and some gold trinkets. Some people told us that a firstborn girl would receive the same gifts; others told us that a firstborn girl received gifts only if she was the firstborn child (and proof of her mother's capability); still others told us that girls received only token gifts of a single outfit of clothes.

Whatever the sex of the child she produces, the new mother has earned herself the right to a month of better than average food. At a bare minimum she must be given two chickens cooked in sesame oil and wine—roosters if she has borne a girl and hens if a boy. The increased intake of protein probably has some effect on the quality or even quantity of the mother's milk, but in this instance it is the mother's health that is considered at stake. Several old women told us that the source of their current aches and pains was the cruel mother-in-law who denied them their chickens after childbirth. Stories illustrating greediness speak of selfish visitors who eat the new mother's chicken, and terrible poverty is poverty so extreme that the new mother's chicken must be bought with borrowed money. Chicken in Taiwanese has the same sound as a word for family (*ke*) and is used symbolically in many contexts. No matter what other delicacies a family may or may not be able to offer a son's wife, when she presents it with a descendant, the family owes her a share of *ke*, literally and symbolically.

As we shall see in Chapter 8, the dominant theme of the marriage ritual is fertility and descendants. There is an extraordinary hunger for descendants among the Taiwanese, and yet their birth is considered unclean and actually dangerous to others. The room in which a birth took place is ritually dirty for a full month and contaminates anyone who enters it. Anyone who has visited such a room must avoid temples, firewalkings, and other activities involving the gods. The new mother is totally contaminated. We were told in Peihotien that she should not set foot outside the house, but if she absolutely has to, she must carry an umbrella or wear a large hat to hide herself from Thi:-kong, the highest god. Many people also believe that if a woman "within the month" enters a building, such as a shop, she must come back after death to wash the threshold. The source of the "dirt" is apparently the postpartum discharge, which in its similarity to the menstrual flow becomes laden with similar taboos (see Chapter 6). Although the postpartum discharge rarely lasts for a full month, a month has become the standard period for ritual uncleanness, regardless of the duration of the flow. A few informants told us that if the child born was a boy, only the mother was unclean, and the visitors to her room would not suffer the same restrictions as they would had the child been a girl. Others denied this. Some said that "the month" was only twenty-nine days for a girl baby and thirty days for a boy baby, the boy having a "more expensive fate" and therefore being more troublesome. The "month" is concluded with several little rituals. Some families roll a hard-cooked chicken egg over the child's face so that it will have a pleasant egg shape and roll a duck egg over the baby's body so it will be long like a duck's and plump like a duck's egg. One woman told us a bit of the yolk of the egg was then put on the child's fontanels, though she did not know why. On the last day of the month either a feast is given for all those who gave presents to the child or gifts of food and rice bowls are sent to them symbolizing a feast. Finally, the child is ritually cleansed of the dirt she got from passing through "the dirty part of a woman" by having her head and eyebrows shaved.*

For the first six weeks of life, a Taiwanese infant spends most of her time on the family bed or in a wheeled bamboo

---

* Since this is a book about females, I am going to use "she" in place of the conventional "he" for the general third-person singular from now on. This should not be taken to mean that the custom under discussion is peculiar to females. When a custom is confined to one sex, I will use the appropriate gender, but for general statements about the treatment of both sexes the "she" seems less misleading.

crib that can be rolled about the house. It is considered dangerous for an infant to be carried too much before she is at least six weeks old. After that she is tied on her mother's back with a long strip of cloth that crisscrosses both of their bodies and in effect swaddles the child. Unfortunately, it provides no support for the infant's rubbery neck. I find the sight of these delicate little heads bobbing loosely very distressing, but Taiwanese mothers assured me it did not matter a bit. Infants, and all babies in cool weather, are further secured with a rectangular cloth that gives a bit more support to their heads. Until they are six or seven months, babies are primarily on their mothers' or grandmothers' backs; only older babies are trusted to the uncertainties of sibling responsibility.

We asked forty-one mothers, "Do you think crying hurts a baby or do you think that it doesn't matter?" Twenty-three of the mothers felt that crying not only did not matter but in some ways was even beneficial. Five of the "pro-crying" mothers felt that crying was a form of infant exercise; five others quoted a proverb to the effect that a child must cry to grow; one mother quoted her grandmother, who had claimed that crying made a child's intestines large, apparently a desirable trait. Seven other women said they did not think crying really harmed a child, but that it bothered them because they felt the child must be uncomfortable. Eleven mothers felt that crying was not good for babies and gave some interesting reasons. Two of them feared that with the child's mouth open so much she might catch cold more easily, and another insisted that crying babies swallowed air and vomited. Crying was particularly dangerous for boys, according to one mother, because it caused their testicles to swell. Another mother said there were only two reasons why a healthy, well-fed baby cried: either she had been frightened or she had "lost her soul." The distinction between these two possibilities is blurry, since a common cause of "soul loss" is a fright. Soul loss is one of the hazards of childhood, a hazard that can be fatal. One of our neighbor's children in Peihotien lost his soul after he was frightened by fireworks, putting the family to great expense. Another child met a ghost who took his soul and returned it only after the intervention of a Taoist priest (and several visits to a local medical doctor).

Toilet training is not something that arouses much concern or interest among Taiwanese mothers. The intimate contact between mother and child during the first few months allows the mother to "know" her baby very well. Mothers claim to be able to identify the restless movements the child makes before she urinates and to use this signal to spread the child's legs and hold her away from their own body. The mother accompanies this act with a whistling noise so that in time the child associates the sound with the activity and empties her bladder on command. Diapers are used only at night, and many mothers claim even these can be dispensed with after six weeks. Mothers say they can keep a dry bed by holding the baby over the edge several times each night (the advantage of earth or concrete floors) and whistling. Bowel control is equally undramatic. When a child can walk she is encouraged to go to a garbage heap or drainage ditch. Accidents are not punished, unless one counts the looks of disgust by an older sister who has to clean it up. Undoubtedly the great number of acceptable toilet areas takes the emotional pressure off both mother and child.

Unless a mother has just fed her child, her almost automatic reaction to a crying baby is to offer her breast. At night the infant shares the same quilt with her mother so that she may nurse at will. Some mothers claim their children receive nothing but mother's milk until they are six months old "because they can't chew," but most village women say even infants are given sips of congee (rice gruel), and I have seen grand-mothers and other substitute caretakers giving babies small mouthfuls of food that they had carefully chewed for them. It seemed to me that even though babies are offered the breast as soon as they cry, by the time they are weaned they are getting the majority of their nourishment from the table. However, even if their diet is perfectly satisfactory in terms of nutrition, the fact that they are still offered the breast when distressed preordains a difficult weaning. When the mother decides the time has come, she simply tells the child her breast is dirty, smearing black bean paste on it; or that it is bloody, smearing it with lipstick; or that it is full of worms. If the child persists in attempts to get at the breast, the mother smears her nipple with pepper and allows the child to nurse. Once or twice is usually sufficient. Thereafter when the child cries unhappily she is offered a biscuit or piece of candy to suck, a transfer that may account for the almost pathological demands of even well-fed village children for money to buy biscuits and candies. At weaning the child is given a new sleeping partner—a grandmother if the youngster is lucky, a father if he is patient, an older sibling if one is available. Mothers claim that their children "forget" in a few days, but our observations of some of these sad little creatures suggest that it was more like a few weeks. At least two mothers admitted that they had tried and failed to wean their babies (both boys) at what was considered an appropriate time. They were finally shamed into self-weaning by their playmates. One skinny little boy, the only child of a couple who had lost two other children, was still nursing at five years.

Nearly every mother we talked to told us that she weaned her daughters a couple of months earlier than her sons. The average age of weaning for boys is seventeen months and for girls, fifteen months, but even mothers who vary from the average maintain the sex differences. For example, a woman who weaned her son at twenty months weaned her daughter at seventeen months. One is tempted to jump to the conclusion that this is an example of preferential treatment of males, but mothers, both those in Peihotien and those in the Sanhsia area, give quite a different reason. They firmly believe that "early" weaning will bring their girls to an early menopause, freeing them of the two-year round of childbirth and the monthly inconvenience of menstruation. What appears to be the acceptance of a male-oriented custom is actually a subversive act by the female culture to benefit the daughters.

In Peihotien we were told of numerous incidents in the early lives of our neighbors that illustrate the once-precarious situation of a female infant. A family in serious need of money sometimes hired out a woman who had just given birth to a girl child as a wet nurse, leaving her own baby to survive or die on congee. In other cases illnesses contracted by girls were approached with a wait-and-see attitude, whereas similar illnesses in their brothers received prompt treatment. In modern Taiwan preferential treatment on such a basic level is uncommon, in part because poverty is less devastating now and in part because of changing attitudes toward human life and suffering, male or female. I have no doubt that if parents had a sick boy and a sick girl and could buy medicine for only one, their choice would be the same as that of their parents and grandparents, but if only the daughter was sick, she would be cared for without hesitation.

A girl's position in her sibling order has a tremendous influence on the quality of her childhood and the alternatives open to her as an adult. In fact, for both boys and girls the comfort of their first few years is dictated by their sibling order. Even a "worthless girl" born into a household without other children is going to be on someone's back or in someone's arms all of her waking and a good many of her sleeping moments. The moment she cries her mother is going to offer her breast or, if she has just been fed, dance her about. Grandparents—and both grandmother and grandfather are likely to be alive and living in the house of a first- or second-born child—will compete to wheedle a smile from her, and her father will wander about the village paths of an evening with his tiny daughter on one arm. But the little girl (and to an only slightly lesser degree the little boy) who is preceded by four or five siblings is in for a childhood with less adult attention and more caretaking by older siblings. If she has the good fortune to be born into a family that lives in a compound or near other similarly constituted families, she may have a group of toddlers to play with, but much of her first few years will be spent tagging along behind an older sister (or less commonly an older brother), too young to participate in her older sibling's games and too big to be long tolerated on her back.

When the older children are off at school, small groups of preschool children play games imitative of their older siblings: two or three hop excitedly, if randomly, through the squares of a hopscotch court drawn by an older group the evening before; another handful makes mud cakes and cooks flowers in the scraps of crockery collected by their siblings the previous afternoon; and precocious little boys play a gambling game with a bunch of cards an elder brother hid carelessly before he left for school. By the time little boys are five years old, the teasing of school-age children (who are segregated from the opposite sex by the school system) forces them to form separate play groups. The girls have less choice in the matter, since many of them have younger brothers trailing behind them whom they dare not exclude.

At some time during a child's early years her eight characters are given to a fortuneteller for his examination. Particularly cautious parents may take a girl child's eight characters to him within a few days of her birth, so that if he finds the particular combination of date and hour of birth have bad portents or will be difficult to match (with a prospective bride-groom's eight characters), the child's characters can be "ad-justed" before registering the birth with the Household Registration Office. By far the most frequent cause for a trip to the fortuneteller is that the child is *kui khi* (expensive, i.e., difficult to raise) and the parents fear she may be *kui mia:* (expensively fated). A child who has frequent though not necessarily serious illnesses, is troublesome, quarrelsome, forever getting into trouble, falling into drainage ditches, tearing her clothes, and in general occupying more of her parents' attention than her siblings is frequently labeled *kui khi*. The state is apparently impermanent. For example, a pregnant woman is warned not to fondle other people's children lest she make them *kui khi*, and it is expected that a woman's own young children will be *kui khi* while she is pregnant. A common diagnosis by fortunetellers of little girls who are *kui khi* is that they have "adopted daughter fates." Several women told us, their voices filled with resentment, that this was the reason their parents had given them away; and others told us the reason they have a "dry mother" (similar to the Western godmother) is that their parents did not wish to give them away in adoption even though a fortuneteller said they were *kui khi* because they had "adopted daughter fates."

The real worry of parents who take their troublesome children to a fortuneteller is that the child might be *kui mia:*. As one woman explained to us, "Not all *kui khi* children are *kui mia:*, but all *kui mia:* children are *kui khi*." A child with an "expensive fate" is both blessed and cursed. If her condition is not recognized and certain precautions taken, she (and girls seem to be as commonly afflicted as boys) may very well die. Moreover, she is a danger to her parents, whom she should address as Uncle and Aunt. If the child does manage to survive the difficult childhood of the *kui mia:*, she is promised a prosperous and happy adulthood. An old lady told us of her troubles with a *kui mia:* granddaughter:

The way we found out she was *kui mia:* was like this. The people next door had a death, and we helped them with the feast. My daughter-in-law ate some of the food too. Later, when she came to feed A-hong, the baby began to scream. Every time her mother offered her the breast she would cry and scream. Finally after two days we took her to the gods, and they said she was *kui mia:*. When we went to the fortuneteller he told us she was *very kui mia:*. We had to feed her powdered milk, which was very expensive in those days, because from then on she wouldn't take her mother's milk. The fortuneteller told us that she must not eat any food from weddings or engagements or funerals, and she must not go to any of these things or even to a temple until she was grown. After that, whenever there was a wedding or a funeral near us, I would hide her in the corner of a bedroom. I couldn't even go to Peikang to worship Ma-co until she was grown. We spent so much money on her! Once a neighbor who had been to a wedding of a relative picked her up, and A-hong was sick for weeks. We spent all our time running back and forth to the gods. Doctors can't help. But now she is grown, and there is no more trouble.

Parents of a child who is prone to illness but not really *kui mia:* often approach a woman who has successfully reared several healthy children and ask her to take their daughter as a "dry daughter." After a minor ritual and the exchange of gifts, the "dry mother" and her new daughter assume a mock parent-child relationship. In effect this amounts to little more than the "dry mother" including the child in family events like marriages, birthday celebrations, and feasts during religious festivals, and the child giving her "dry mother" little gifts and paying her visits. In some cases as the child grows older she outgrows the relationship and has little more to do with her "dry mother" than she does with other women. Often, however, a warm bond of affection develops between the "dry mother" and her charge, and the tie that was merely formal becomes real, lasting until death. In asking about the "dry mother" relationship in Peihotien, we discovered that it was not always initiated by the parents of an ailing child. Sometimes a woman who has a favorite among the children of a friend asks to be made her "dry mother." One woman in Peihotien who had the misfortune to never bear children of her own had at least two "dry daughters" that we knew of; now adults, they were still frequent visitors to her home. We also found several cases in which older women who had become particularly fond of village teen-agers (and in one case of a young bride) formalized their relationships by referring to themselves and their favorites as "dry mother" and "dry daughter."

Taiwanese parents assume that children cannot really "understand" until they are around six years old. They claim that until then they do not try to teach them anything and expect little in the way of obedience. At the most they hope the preschool child will not injure herself or cause her parents too much trouble. Obviously even such a low level of expectation requires some socialization on the parents' part, and actually a good deal of training goes on before a child enters school. It is here that the difference in training given boys and girls begins to emerge, particularly for little girls who have younger siblings. It is not unusual for a four-year-old girl to be put in charge of her two-year-old brother, though the mother will insist that both stay within her hearing range. Parents may think they do not "expect" obedience of preschool children, but a mother will severely scold or even beat a four-year-old girl who does something that endangers her small brother. At first a little girl learns which games she dares play with little brother on her back simply by finding out which ones she does not get scolded or slapped for playing, but it does not take long for a child of average intelligence to figure out the hazards of various games. Thus, by the time a girl is of school age she has had much more responsibility training than her male counterpart. She has also learned the pain that follows disobedience, and a few of the ways to avoid that pain.

Beyond learning a few chores and some of the behavior that pleases adults, such as obedience, a preschool Taiwanese girl learns her first subtle lessons about the second-class status of her sex. She has heard from the time she could understand words that she was a "worthless girl," though the tone of voice may often have been consoling. The older she gets, however, the more often she will be involved in incidents like this one, culled from our child observations. Wan-iu: (a four-year-old girl) was sitting on a small stool near the well. A neighbor came out and said, "Wan-iu:, let Thiam-hok (a two-and-a-half-year-old boy) sit on your stool so he won't get dirty." Wan-iu: pushed him away and said, "No, you can't have my stool. Get away." Wan-iu:'s mother shouted at her angrily, "You are a girl! Give him that stool. I'll beat you to death!" Wan-iu: looked unhappy but gave up the stool. This little girl had no brothers, or she probably would never have gotten into this kind of trouble. By age five most little girls have learned to step aside automatically for boys, at least when their parents are watching. Little girls who have younger siblings of either sex have explored many techniques for fulfilling their responsibilities to their parents' satisfaction and still joining in the village play groups. Threatening or hitting little brother when he wants to do something other than hang around big sister's playmates is early discovered to be a technique that will result in quick and often painful punishment. A favorite parental ploy is to promise young children a special treat of food or an outing to get them to run an errand or do a chore. Even the parents admit they rarely fulfill these promises, claiming that the children forget about them anyway. This seems to be one of the first successful techniques that little girls imitate. We have heard many a four- or five-year-old girl solemnly promising to take her two-year-old brother on a trip to Taipei if he will just sit quietly through one more turn in the jump rope contest.

Whether or not the age at which parents expect their children to suddenly become obedient, responsible, and helpful, and the age at which they first attend school are anything other than coincident is moot. In the past this was the age at which girls gave up their freedom of movement by having their feet bound. The demands made on modern children of both sexes at this age, both in the harsh environment of the school and at home, are immense, and for lack of any initiation are probably more traumatic for boys than for girls. Little girls who have been caring for a younger brother or sister for a year or two have already discovered the price of disobedience. More important, they have become sensitive to subtleties like tone of voice and setting that indicate which commands require immediate obedience, which can be delayed, and which can be ignored. Their male peers must learn these lessons in a very brief period, and to make matters worse, they are taught both by a demanding teacher (in a foreign language) and by an unexpectedly demanding parent. Little boys whose disobedience was a source of amusement or at most brought a laughing swat suddenly find themselves hit with a ruler for not sitting down when told to. Fathers who used to be affectionate become distant, with a tendency to lecture. Taiwanese parents believe that if they are "friends" to their children they will not be able to "teach" them. When their sons reach the age of "reason," fathers must withdraw to become dignified disciplinarians. Although many people told us that mothers should be less affectionate with children after this age also, it is difficult for a mother to maintain a cool dignity while scrubbing dirty ears. Still, when we asked a mother if it was all right to let children see that you are fond of them, she answered: "You musn't let children see that you like them. That way it is easier to teach them. If there is even one person in a family who spoils the children you just won't be able to teach them anything. Children's eyes are very sharp. If they know there is someone in the family like that, then they will go ahead and do anything because they can always run to that person and be safe."

One day in a casual conversation we asked a father if it was a good thing to praise children. He replied: "Well, people here say you have to divide it into two parts. When children are little you should praise them, and they will be happy and do what you want. But you should not do this when they are older or else they will think, 'I'm good enough,' and then they will think they can get away with something bad." A mother in response to a similar question said: "I praise her but not to her face. You cannot let children know that you approve of them. If they know that you praise them, they won't try to improve." For village parents, praise is simply not considered a technique for training children. It is an indication of weakness in a parent, weakness that may well ruin the children. The basic philosophy of socialization among farmers seems to be that if you wish to train a child, the child must fear you. The only way to encourage *desired* behavior is to punish *undesired* behavior severely. As one mother said, "Do you think that they will listen to you when you scold them? What good does that do? All you can do is grab one and really hit him hard. Then the others will be good too. You know the saying, 'If the children in the upper house are getting beaten, the children in the lower house will be good.'" Most parents feel that physical punishment is necessary to motivate learning. When we admired the ability of the storekeeper's eight-year-old son to make change, the mother told us how the boy's father had taught him. "One day someone came to buy something and my son figured and figured, but he couldn't figure out how much money to give the man in change. His father got mad and hit him. Then he took some money and showed the boy how to do it. He questioned him to see if he understood, and when he didn't he got hit again. After that his father questioned him all the time and hit him whenever he answered wrong. He knows now."

Most mothers were frank in their responses to our questions about physical punishment, a frankness that I fear may no longer be possible now that national television is spreading information about other people's values. A typical response to a question about the acceptability of physical punishment was: "It depends on the mother's character. Some mothers prefer to hit children and others to explain to them. I prefer to hit them." Only one mother out of the forty-one asked felt that children do not benefit by being "hit." She said: "Whether a child is good or not is determined at its birth. So hitting a child is of no use. In the old days people liked to beat their children to death [i.e., excessively], but this is of no use. If you beat a thief, he still steals, so what use is there in beating him? You explain the reasons for things to good children, and they will understand. If they are bad, they won't be good even if you do beat them." The forty mothers who were in favor of physical punishment qualified their answers with statements ranging from the quite mild ("I think the less you punish, the better. If you hit him in the afternoon and again in the evening, he won't be afraid of you and will be even naughtier.") to the more rigid ("Children ought to be hit. It does them no harm.").

A beating administered by a Taiwanese parent is often severe, leaving the child bruised and in some cases bleeding. Parents prefer to use a bamboo rod to discipline children, but they will use their hand or fist if there is no bamboo available, and if they are really angry, they will pick up whatever is at hand. Crueler forms of physical punishment are also used by a few parents, such as making the offending child kneel on the ridged surface of an abacus or tying the child in a dark corner. One mother was pointed out to us who had recently punished her son by tying his wrists, throwing the rope over a beam, and drawing it up enough to keep him standing on his toes. Most parents find such techniques too harsh. The most frequent physical punishment is simply an irritated slap applied to whatever part of the anatomy the mother can reach, but we witnessed or heard of at least one severe beating every few days when we lived in Peihotien.

Mothers say that most severe beatings come about when the children make them so angry they cannot stop hitting them. When the *khi*, or steam, builds up within a person it must be released, just as steam cannot be allowed to build up in a boiler lest it cause an explosion. If the *khi* in a human is not released it will eventually result in physical or mental illness. If the cause for the buildup of *khi* is removed, it will dissipate just as steam in a boiler will, once the heat has been removed. One woman told us when we asked her what she did if her child ran away while she was punishing him: "Oh, when your *khi* is high you beat them if you can catch them, but if you wait awhile your *khi* goes out and you forget about it." When we asked another mother if she stopped hitting her children when they started to cry, she answered: "I still hit them after they begin to cry because I am very mad, and I go on hitting them until I'm not mad anymore."

Mothers recognize that punishment administered in a fit of temper can sometimes endanger their children. The following conversation took place between a group of mothers. One of the children was being naughty, and her mother grabbed her and hit her quite hard in the middle of the back. Another woman, Kim-lan, chided the mother. "How can you hit a child there? You're as bad as Phik-gioq, you never look before you hit." The mother laughed and said, "I never do. When

I'm mad how can I look? I just hit them wherever I can with whatever I have in my hand. If I waited to find a stick, they could do anything." A-mui, another mother in the group, admitted, "I'm that way too. You have to hit them when you are mad, or they will run off and you'll forget about it. Like yesterday. I finished cooking about four-thirty. The youngest wanted to eat so I gave her something. Then all the others [five of them] came around yelling, wanting to eat too. I was so hot and so mad that I just grabbed the oldest one and beat her up. I think I really hurt her, but they made me so mad I just grabbed the closest one and hit her, and then they were all quiet." Kim-lan said, "That is why everyone says, 'If the children in the upper house are getting beaten, the children in the lower house will be good.'" A-mui agreed, "That's the way it was. I just beat the oldest one, and the others were very quiet and ate their rice and went outside. They didn't bother me anymore." Our research assistant asked, "Can't you just scold them and tell them not to do it?" A-mui laughed. "What good would that do? All you can do is hit one. Do you think they will listen to you if you just scold them?"

Ordinarily, outsiders would not dare interfere in a "family" affair, but anyone, even a stranger, is expected to interfere when a mother clearly has lost control of her temper while beating a child. If this was not an accepted custom, there would be many more severely battered children in the villages than there are. We observed the following scene in one of the yards in Peihotien. Ai-cu, a little girl of seven years, grabbed a rice cake away from her younger sister, and the younger child began to cry. Their mother came out of the house and hit Ai-cu, saying, "This girl! Why couldn't you just wait a few seconds. She would have given you some." The mother grabbed the cake away from Ai-cu and began slapping her very hard on the face. After she slapped her several times, she said, "The more I think about you the madder I get." She hit her on the chin with her fist quite hard and said, "I don't know how many times I have scolded you for being a hungry ghost." The old woman who was selling the cakes said to the mother, "All right. All right. Let's forget about it now. You have already hit her and so next time she will remember." The old lady pushed Ai-cu away, telling her, "Now next time you had better not do that, little girl." As she said this, the old lady grabbed the mother's hand to keep her from hitting Ai-cu again. The mother yelled a few curses at Ai-cu and then walked away. Ai-cu stood under a tree sobbing, with the blood running down her chin from a cut on her lip. Although in this case it was a stranger who came to the child's rescue, more often it is a member of the family who ends such beatings. Even an older sibling, who under other circumstances would be in serious trouble for interfering with an adult activity, is expected to pull away a child whose mother has "lost control" in the midst of a beating.

It is almost always the mother who administers these severe beatings, which are often the result of a final irritation in a day of too many children wanting too much attention all at the same time. (The women's behavior is strikingly similar to the frantic temper tantrums preschool children indulge in after some minor frustration that is the final blow in a day of denials.) A child's adult siblings or her father's brothers and their wives may occasionally restrain her from performing a misdeed or even scold her, but they rarely go so far as to slap a child not their own. Grandparents have the authority to punish and do not hesitate to do so if they want to, but grandparents rarely want anything beyond affection from their grandchildren. Grandparents have less to fear from a badly raised grandchild, i.e., they do not risk an uncomfortable old age because of an unfilial child, and are inclined to want to "enjoy" their grandchildren as they did not dare enjoy their own children. Consequently, they frequently make the job of the parents difficult, since the children soon discover the hierarchy of authority in the family and the inclination of grandmother to intercede whenever mother threatens to withhold dinner or refuses a candy.

Oddly enough, it is not mother, the most frequent and often the most violent punisher, the children most fear, but father. Ideally, fathers never punish in anger. A child is brought before father as a culprit before a magistrate. An appropriate number of blows is administered—with disapproval but without passion. From the looks on the children's faces, these blows are far more painful than mother's in her greatest fury. Mother, of course, encourages this attitude toward father, both as a disciplinary convenience and as a way of strengthening the bonds that unite her uterine family. Father's distance and the fact that *he* can beat mother (and Taiwanese children have witnessed such events) make him appear to be a tremendously powerful being who is known to punish but rarely to pardon. Mother, in contrast, punishes frequently and pardons even more frequently.

A crying baby is quickly tended to make sure she is neither hungry nor in pain, and when it is only a matter of frustration, the mother tries to distract her if she cannot remove the frustration. Child caretakers also learn to indulge their charges to stop the noise and, as the case may be, keep out of trouble. The response to an older child's crying is often devoid of what we call nurturant behavior. In fact, nurturant comforting behavior is rarely seen in Taiwanese families except toward the very young. Older children learn not to ask for sympathy and to endure a variety of pains without displaying the emotions we usually recognize as requests for comforting, supportive behavior from their parents. A school-age child who falls and scrapes her knee knows better than to come and ask a parent for help. One mother told us: "They don't dare come crying to me. I always scold them and say, 'I called you to help me

73

so why didn't you come instead of staying there and getting yourself hurt.' Or else I say, 'Why didn't you stay home? Why do you have to go outside and play and get hurt?' Really, sometimes they get bad scrapes, but they never tell me about it. They go and get some medicine and put it on themselves. Anyway, they are this old now [seven and nine years] so they shouldn't come crying to me." Displays of affection, except toward infants, are frowned on in Taiwanese society, and perhaps nurturant behavior is too similar in appearance to be socially acceptable. The traditional belief that a child's body belongs to her parents, and any injury to it an affront to them, produces what appears to be very callous behavior on the part of parents. Cui-tho, a ten-year-old boy, was squatting down in the road looking at his finger, which was deeply cut and bleeding profusely. He had cut it trying to split a piece of bamboo with a razor blade. His mother came out of the house, noticed him, and asked, "Well, what are you supposed to be doing? Have you finished yet?" Cui-tho was supposed to be sweeping the yard in preparation for the police inspection. He got up right away and went back to his sweeping. His mother saw the blood running down his hand and asked, "What's wrong with your hand?" He answered, "Nothing." His mother shouted at him, "Let me see it." He held his hand out, and she asked angrily, "How did you do it?" Cui-tho turned away without answering, going back to his work. His mother turned to us and said, "He probably was being 'busy' and cut himself. Serves him right."

Aggression is a facet of children's behavior that worries all adults. Every member of the family is concerned to keep it at a minimum. Squabbling children can lead to quarrels between adults, and important adult relationships can become endangered over an incident that began with two four-year-olds and one rubber band. Already strained relations between adult brothers can be brought to the point of household division if a child's quarrel is allowed to exacerbate adult tensions. Even grandparents who are happy to indulge their descendants in everything else frown on quarrels within their family and are troubled by a child who is frequently reported as involved in a neighborhood fracas. And the young mother has her own reasons for wanting to keep her youngster's aggression within acceptable bounds. By the time her children are wandering about the village paths, she has carefully built up friendships with other village women. She depends heavily on these friendships for advice, sympathy, small loans, and should the need arise, a social forum in which to try her mother-in-law's treatment of her. In the early years of her marriage they are her only support, and she cannot afford to have them endangered by naughty children.

When we interviewed mothers about their children's aggression, we were not surprised to find that they condemned it. We asked, "If your child is playing with one of the other children in the neighborhood and there is a quarrel or fight, how do you handle it?" Only two mothers felt that merely separating the children was sufficient. Sixteen mothers said they would find out who was in the wrong and punish their child if she was responsible. Twenty-three mothers, however, said they asked no questions but simply called the child home and scolded her for getting involved in a fracas, no matter who started it. "I always call my children home and scold them first. Then I ask them why. If they say other children hit them first, I ask them, 'Why did they hit you? If you didn't provoke them, why would they hit you?' If my child is really in the right, I may tell the other child that if he does it again I will report it to his mother. If my child hit the other child, I will scold my child and tell the other one that when my child's father comes home he will beat him. That will comfort the other child."

No matter what aspect of child training we discussed with

mothers the conversation always turned to the control of aggression. When we asked a mother to describe a good child, the first characteristic was always "one who does not get into fights." When we asked questions we assumed to be totally irrelevant to aggression, such as, "If another child falls down should your child go and help him?," we were given answers like, "No, because someone will say they were fighting, and he will get into trouble." We asked forty-two mothers a series of questions about play behavior: whether they preferred to have their children play in groups or alone, at home or away from home, and the like. Twenty-nine of the mothers answered one or more of these questions with, "It doesn't matter as long as they don't fight."

Thirty-four out of thirty-nine mothers denied that they ever told their children to hit back when attacked, and indeed some of the mothers were indignant at our asking such a question. The other five mothers were not quite so rigid in their answers, one of them saying, "To tell the truth, I would tell my girl to hit back, but I always tell her, 'You must not hit first. If he hits you and you can't get away, hit him back.' They are all children, and I can't let my child be bullied outside by others." When we asked the other mothers just what they told their children to do when attacked by other children, twenty-four said they told their children to come home, five admitted they would scold the other child, and seven mothers said they would call their own children home and punish them for getting themselves into a situation where they were aggressed against. Our observations of play behavior around the village, much of it within earshot of parents, only partly confirm these answers. If the children get into a fracas that is noisy or lasts more than a few seconds or comes to the attention of other adults, I think mothers quickly intervene. But most of the time they are far too busy to notice what the various play groups are up to. Probably aggression that occurs in the house between siblings or playmates is quickly punished. "Outside" aggression is punished only when brought to the parents' attention. Since girls are more likely to be within sight and sound of their mothers than boys, they receive more consistent punishment for expressing aggression. This and the fact that they are generally less active than boys may account for their reputation of being less aggressive.

Even though mothers tell their children to come home if someone attacks them, a child cannot count on her reception if she comes home with a report of a neighbor child's assault. A mother who is anxious about her relations in the village may give the child a slap for getting herself involved in an aggressive situation. Children learn quite early that if they cannot be sure of winning the battle without adult intervention, the best place to go is to the attacker's mother. Most mothers respond promptly by grabbing their child and, to use the village expression, "beat her for you to watch." Even if the child cannot be caught, her victim can be fairly sure she will have trouble when she does come home. The complaint of one's own child can be ignored, but the complaint of a friend's child is a serious matter that threatens adult relations if not quickly dealt with.

Unfortunately, the techniques used to punish aggression in children seem only to provide adult models of the same behavior. The furious mother beating a child is a clear example of an adult indulging in a kind of behavior that is labeled "bad." An aggressed-against child is comforted by being told that the aggressor will be beaten, and that she will have the *pleasure* of witnessing the assault. There are numerous situations where a child is comforted with this thought. The message the child receives about aggression is at best unclear. She is told she must not hit other children, but experience tells her that she had better not let other children know they can hit her with impunity. She is told that aggression is bad, but her reward for abstaining is to watch someone else being beaten. What the rule must come down to is simply: if you want one of your peers hit, try first to get someone else to do it for you, but if you have to do it yourself, do not get caught.

In view of the traditional Chinese concern with filiality and adults' frequent statements of anxiety about who will care for them in their old age, we assumed obedience would be a trait that Taiwanese parents felt strongly about. And the mothers' responses to our questions seem to confirm this. Thirty-eight out of forty-one said that they expected their children to obey immediately and that they would not countenance dawdling. Thirty-five said they would hit or scold a child who dawdled. But when we went on to ask the same mothers if they always insisted that the child obey their orders even if the child did not want to, thirty-one admitted they would just let the matter go. Clearly, the ideal is the child who jumps up and immediately does whatever her mother asks, but many mothers admit and our own observations verify that obedience often comes at too high a price. Busy mothers find it quicker and less frustrating to do the job themselves, particularly in the case of preschool children. The different expectations with regard to obedience and age are nicely illustrated in the following observation. He-iam, a four-year-old boy, was sitting on a stool doing nothing. His mother came out and asked him urgently to go next door and get some medicine for her to put on the baby, who had bumped his head rather badly. He-iam said loudly, "No, I won't." The mother said, "Please go and get it. Go." She pinched him on the knee when he still did not move, and he cursed her and continued to refuse. Just then He-iam's older brother came up, a boy of seven in his first year of school, and the mother asked him to go. He went off at a run.

If the disobedient child in the above observation had been a girl, she would not have been so arrogant in her refusal.

Obedience training comes earlier for girls than for boys, less by plan than by the accident of role requirements. A child who must be responsible for a younger child's welfare cannot be allowed to disobey on whim. Moreover, the cost of obtaining submission is not as high in a daughter. Obedience is behavior mothers plainly find desirable in all their children, but they find the training to secure it, particularly in their sons, too threatening to relationships they value more. Fathers depend on filiality (and children certainly obey their fathers' commands more readily than they do those of their mothers), but mothers depend on the bonds of sentiment. When the naughty behavior of their sons threatens their important relations in the women's community, they will punish them without question; when the disobedient behavior of their sons interferes with their routines or threatens the values of the male concept of filiality, they will let it pass. Mothers respond to questionnaires in terms of what they know to be the culture's ideals and the needs of the men's families, but their behavior reflects their own best interests and the needs of the uterine families. Their futures depend on the quality of their relations with their sons.

⚙ 6 ⚘

Older Girls

Some Taiwanese girls attended primary school during the Japanese period, but it is really only in the last twenty years that compulsory primary education was thought to apply to girls as well as boys. Most parents now seem content to have their girls in school, and even the most conservative have come to accept the propriety of having their daughters taught in the same room with boys from other families. In Peihotien in 1958 there were only three or four school-age girls who were not in school. As far as most families are concerned, school is learning to read and write, and although these skills are more necessary for boys than girls, they can be useful to girls. Except for political propaganda, the values the schools teach would probably be quite acceptable to most village parents if they were even aware that their children were being taught such things. Obedience, propriety, perseverance, respect for seniors—all are appropriate goals for both boys and girls. Girls who also learn that they can outdo the majority of their classmates, including those superior male beings, on most tests may develop a taste for the world beyond the village that will cause them and their families a bit of trouble, but not enough to concern unaffected parents. In general, school is a good thing.

To the child, however, a Chinese country schoolroom must seem a forbidding place. Floors are cement, walls are dirty plaster, and the furniture makes no allowance for the natural curves of the body. Lighting is minimal. School budgets, including teachers' salaries, are disgracefully low. In 1958 the playground at Tapu District School had only three swings and two rickety teeter-totters for five hundred students. The yard was hard-packed dirt, dusty in the dry season and impossibly muddy in the wet season. The drab environment was relieved only by the bright Nationalist flag and the occasionally refreshed (by paint only) political slogans adorning the walls. Books, paper, and pencils are paid for by the parents, and for some families even these few dollars become a drain on their limited resources. The parents must also provide uniforms for their children, dark blue skirts and white blouses for the girls, khaki pants and shirts for the boys. One mother in Peihotien told us: "Gioq-hiou is an adopted daughter, so I have to let her go to school or everyone would gossip about us. It costs so much for us to keep her in school that if she were my own child I wouldn't let her continue. It doesn't do any good for a girl to study anyway. They study, but it is still the same for them after."

At Tapu District School all the children are expected to be in their classrooms at 7:30 each morning. The teachers make some introductory remarks, collect money, and then go off to a teachers' meeting, leaving the students in charge of student leaders. These monitors are chosen on the basis of good marks, good behavior, and according to some young cynics, the importance of their parents in the community. They are usually male. When the teachers return from their meeting, the third- through sixth-grade classes line up in the yard for an address by the principal, the singing of the national anthem, and group calisthenics. The principal's address ranges from simple announcements to lectures on good citizenship and the national effort to resist "Communist bandits." It is also a time when children guilty of a variety of sins are publicly reprimanded. One morning our assistant jotted down the following lecture: "Yesterday I told you all to get to school on time and not be late again. Today I didn't go to the gate until 7:45, but still there were students arriving. All late students step forward. [Some moved forward slowly.] Run! [They ran to the front of the assembly.] About face! Now everyone look at them. One-fifth of the girls are late, and one-third of the boys are late. Look again! There are more big children than little children. These are lazy children. The bigger they are, the more they sleep." The principal's delivery indicated that he expected laughter, and even the offenders had trouble keeping straight faces. Since it was only the second day of school, their only punishment was to clean a small area of the schoolyard, but future latecomers were threatened with cleaning the entire yard, and both actors and audience knew that this would probably be the last time there would be laughter allowed in assembly.

At this same assembly the children who had not brought their book and notebook fees were asked to step forward. All those who promised to bring it next day were then allowed to return to their ranks, and of course all of the children did so. About a week later the children who had not yet paid were again called to the front of the assembly. They made a group of about twenty-five or thirty boys and girls. They were required to face the assembly and then led off in a separate group to the front of the principal's office. There the principal spoke to them. "You have not yet paid your fees. I know you are not really poor. I have been to your *Li Chang* and have found out that your families all contributed at least NT $20 for Tho-te-kong's birthday festival on the first day it was asked for.* I know that your fathers or mothers or even both of them gamble, so they have money, but they don't pay the

* The exchange rate for New Taiwan dollars (NT $) in 1958 was forty to one U.S. dollar.

school. You may pay in three installments as long as the NT $30 is paid by October 5. Go home and tell your parents. Tomorrow you must give me the first installment. If your parents don't give you the money, I am going to take away your things. Altogether this group owes over NT $700. How can the school pay that much? If someone gambles and neither wins nor loses, he must pay at least NT $25 to stay in the game. Why can't he give one night's gambling to the school? Poorer students than you have already paid their fees. There are five of you who cannot pay, and I know that. [Our assistant said that there were at least three children from our village in the group who would have trouble finding the money and not because their parents gambled.] Why can't the rest of you pay? Every family in this district has given the school NT $5 and another NT $2 for flood relief. You are excused from paying this, but you do have to pay the NT $30 for your supplies. [Some of the children were beginning to cry.] I know you want to pay and that it is your parents who won't give you the money, but today you must go home and tell them that they can pay in three installments. Anyone who does not will have to give back his books and notebooks. There is a student who is absent today—his teacher gave him an NT $15 scholarship. He has still not paid either. If he can't get the rest of the money, he can give the NT $15. How can he not? Does he just come to school to get money?" After a few more words, the principal allowed the humiliated children to return to the main assembly and join in the mass calisthenics.

Tapu School has a kindergarten, but when we lived in Peihotien, many parents could see no reason for paying fees to send their preschool children to school for a few hours a day to sing and cut out pictures. We happened to be visiting in a house when a young boy came home from kindergarten. He proudly showed his mother a piano he had learned to make by folding a sheet of paper. The mother glanced at it and said scornfully, "Every day the teacher teaches you these foolish things. 'Wants-to-die!' [a curse]. Making these toys and not teaching you to write words!" For most village parents, school is a place to learn to read and write. The gradual adjustment to school routines, the mild introduction to discipline and to the tools of education, pencil and paper, make kindergarten particularly valuable to the children of uneducated parents, but because of their lack of education, these are precisely the parents who are least likely to understand the need for it. The most painful aspects of a child's first few weeks in school result from unsympathetic teachers and the Chinese philosophy of education, but it is exacerbated by the child's total ignorance of what school is all about and what is expected of him. When we expressed our surprise at seeing about a third of the students of a first-grade class leave the room with red swollen eyes, some still wiping at tears, a vice-principal at Tapu School gave us the following insightful explanation.

Most of these children did not go to kindergarten, and many of them have no older brothers or sisters in school. They have never held a pencil in their hands before today. Many of them come from farm families that may not even own a pencil. When they first pick one up it seems very heavy to them, and they have no idea how to use it. They see other children using them, and they can't. They are angry with themselves because they can't. Also, before they come to school their parents never force them to do anything. When they come to school they *have* to do something for the first time. If they don't the teacher scolds them or hits them until they do. They are mad at themselves because they can't do well and afraid because the teacher will scold them if they don't. All they can do is cry. I've learned, though, that the child who cries in the first grade isn't always the dumb one. Sometimes these are the ones who turn out to be the best students. They are just scared in a new place. If they had gone to kindergarten, much of this would have been avoided.

Despite the difference in culture, the Tapu kindergarten curriculum is not unlike that of a kindergarten in an impoverished area of the United States. The children are taught little ditties that instruct them to wash their hands and cut their fingernails so "the hundred sicknesses" won't come. They are introduced to handkerchiefs and taught to use them. They are taught to stand at the teacher's order, to sit on order, to file out of the classroom on order. They are taught the appropriate response to rhetorical questions such as, "This child has dirty hands. Is this a good child?" or "This morning I heard a mother telling her child to hurry and get up to go to school. The child said, 'No! If you don't give me 50¢ for candy, I won't get up.' Is this a good child?" They learn slowly and sometimes painfully that the school bell rings for them just as it does for their older brothers and sisters. One day during the first week of school we met one of our neighbors on the path. She was half angry and half laughing. One of her friends had noticed her grandson and two other kindergartners from Peihotien wandering around the schoolyard during school hours. The grandmother hurried down to the school and shooed them into their classroom. When we met her she was returning from her second trip for the same purpose. She told us that this time she had turned them over to the teacher and had asked her to please hit them so they would learn what the bell meant. Another mother told us that she was surprised to see her young son walk in the door one morning at about ten o'clock. She asked why he had come home early, and he explained that he was hungry. When his mother returned him to the school, his teacher said he had just gotten up and walked out.

This gentle introduction to an environment that will soon turn very stern and become very demanding is probably the most important function of the kindergarten, but for most parents the only part of the four-hour kindergarten day worth the expense is that in which the children are introduced to

Mandarin, the official language of China. After the first grade children are punished if they are caught speaking their native Taiwanese at school. (This prohibition includes the school-yard, but since teachers seldom appear there, it is rarely enforced directly. Even so, the school atmosphere is so strong that we nearly always heard Mandarin being spoken in the yard, and Taiwanese resorted to only by the very young and by those in need of cursewords.) Obviously, children who learn to speak a few words of Mandarin in kindergarten and to comprehend some of the simple stories told them in Mandarin by their teachers have an initial advantage in the first grade. With some the advantage may be real in that it gives them a confidence they will badly need later. For many, the advantage of a few words of Mandarin amounts only to a technique with which they can impress their parents.

The serious business of school—the harsh discipline, rigid routine, long hours of rote memorization—begins in the first grade. Although today's "modern" schools no longer require children to spend their first few years memorizing classical texts, whose meaning will not be explained until much later, bare literacy cannot be attained without hours of memorization. Chinese scholars take great pride in the subtlety and attendant difficulty of their language; to have the honor of reading it, one must be willing to expend much energy. Perhaps the discipline required to memorize the several thousand characters necessary for newspaper literacy is the origin of the air of rigid discipline that pervades Taiwanese schools. In one of the classrooms my husband observed, the children were expected to sit at all times with their feet flat on the floor, knees together, backs straight, both hands holding their books at a 45-degree angle to the desk. The teacher quite literally shouted commands that would bring the children into or out of this position, cause them to rise in a group, march out of the room in order, and so on. This is a long way for the kindergartner who used to wander home for a mid-morning snack to travel in a year, and for the children who do not go to kindergarten the fall from paradise is instantaneous.

One of our staff members was talking to the grandmother of a young boy who had until recently been the center of every play group and in the midst (if not the cause) of every fight. She asked the woman why she had not seen much of the boy recently. "Well, he has kind of changed. Now he comes home and does his homework before he goes out to play. I guess that is why you don't see much of him. I'm really surprised too. At first I had to call him, but no more, and when I check to see if it is done, it always is. He wasn't that way in kindergarten." She laughed sympathetically. "Poor little boy. Sometimes he askes me to test him on his numbers. I write a number like 39, and then he's supposed to write the next number. Sometimes he forgets, and if I scold him a little he cries and cries. I'm always afraid he will get mad and quit. That's the way he used to be, but now even if he cries he keeps on trying to do it."

Some of the most distressing observations we made on Taiwan came from a first-grade classroom in Tapu School. The short-tempered bitter woman who taught the class is certainly not typical of Taiwan's teachers, but unfortunately she is not that exceptional either. When my assistant was sent to observe the classroom alone (thus disturbing its natural climate somewhat less than I, as a foreigner, would), she found it very difficult to keep from interceding in the children's behalf. When she entered the room, the teacher, Mrs. Li, was yelling at the children, telling them how dumb they were and scolding them for not trying hard enough. Another teacher entered the room with a message, and Mrs. Li told her what a very bad class she had and then pointed out several crying children—hitting them as she pointed them out—that were particularly dumb or bad or both. When Mrs. Li left the room for a meeting a little later, our assistant worked with two children, a boy and a girl, who seemed the most upset, guiding their hands and then praising them when they managed to complete a character on their own. When she observed the class again the next day, she felt that the little girl showed decided improvement, although she still wrote awkwardly. But Mrs. Li either could not or would not take note of the improvement and scolded the child severely for not practicing at home (even though she showed the teacher several pages of "practice work"). The teacher called her a bad girl and told the class (evidently for our assistant's benefit) that the child had run away from school and stayed home for two days because she was afraid to write. All of Mrs. Li's students were terrified of her. They feared what she said, but even more the manner in which she said it. Both first-grade teachers asked their classes each morning if they had remembered to bring their handkerchiefs. In Mrs. Li's room those who had forgotten burst into tears. The other first-grade class received the same scolding, but gentle Mrs. Chang made the oversight seem somewhat less momentous. Nevertheless, even in her classroom the frustrated children attempting to draw their first characters in the squares of their copy books often cried. Unlike Mrs. Li, Mrs. Chang did not shout at the crying children, but she did not give them any extra help either. And if the child was disobedient, he or she could expect to feel the sting of the bamboo stick.

For most children, and particularly for boys, this change from the relatively untrammeled, undisciplined life of the preschooler is bitter and made even more so because it is mirrored in their parents' treatment of them at home. Some children accept the change as they would accept a cloud over the sun, but others find it too difficult to bear. One little girl from Peihotien attended school willingly for the first week and then simply refused to return. She was in Mrs. Li's class, and although we never observed her crying, she looked stunned most of the time. No one in her family was able to read, and consequently her parents were eager for her to learn, but unfortunately they were unable to understand her problem or to help her. Her mother's only solution to the child's rebellion was to beat her into submission, but the little girl preferred the physical punishment to the mental anguish of Mrs. Li's classroom. Finally her grandmother carried her bodily to the school and to the vice-principal. The grandmother's little speech to the vice-principal was pathetic. "She spent all summer playing school. She was so happy to get to go to school. The first day she came home and said she had to have a book bag, so I bought it. Then she had to have a dark skirt and white blouse, so I bought it. And then there was money for books and papers. But no one in our house can read, and her mother wanted so much for her to read. And then yesterday she wouldn't go to school. Her mother beat her, and she ran away. And this morning she wouldn't go, and her mother tied her up and beat her. Still she won't go. Her mother likes her very much and wants her to have a better life." The vice-principal seemed to have no answer for this sincere old woman other than to suggest she promise the child some treat and see if that might help. The grandmother had tried that. Finally the vice-principal suggested that the child be allowed to stay at home for another year, since it is harder on a child who has no older brothers and sisters to adjust to school. The grandmother pointed out that the girl was nearly seven now. Mrs. Chang, the other first-grade teacher (who lives near Peihotien) came up just then and tried to be of help. The vice-principal made good her escape, and Mrs. Chang tried to talk the child into coming with her to her class. The little girl showed some interest in the kindergarten when she discovered one need not learn to write there, but the single kindergarten was already overcrowded. Just as Mrs. Chang and the grandmother got the child to the door of the other first grade, she broke from their grasp and ran out of the schoolyard. Mrs. Chang tried to comfort the old woman, who seemed on the verge of tears herself. The little girl did not return to school that year and made a very lonely figure in the village during school hours.

The use of physical punishment in the schools is rarely objected to by the parents. On the contrary, many parents will complain to the principal if their children do poorly, blaming it on a lack of discipline in the classroom. The teacher who does not hit his students does not care about their welfare and is not fulfilling his responsibilities as a teacher. Learning must be painful. Learning must also be burdensome and take place in part under the eyes of the parents if they are to believe the teacher is doing his duty. Most teachers assign certain lessons as homework and forbid the children to do the work during free periods or study periods at school. For their own protection the teachers must have proof that they made a student work hard in case the student fails in one of the annual examinations.

Many young people whose interests might lead them into becoming teachers are lost to that profession in Taiwan because of the antiquated teaching techniques required by the system; because of the major loss of status for teachers that resulted from the government's early practice of placing all literate but otherwise unemployable mainlanders in the school system; and because of the gross underpayment of teachers that requires them to exploit their students by charging them for tutorial classes—the infamous *pu-hsi-pan*. In 1968 a discouraged young teacher who had just taken a job in business told us:

The primary goal of education in Taiwan is to pass the examinations for lower middle school, then upper middle school, and finally college. Each examination passed gets the student a better job, and good jobs are not easy to find. This is the reason there are so many *pu-hsi-pan*. If a student doesn't get into middle school, he is going to be a coolie or a farmer no matter how smart he is. The competition to get into the right middle schools and the right colleges is so intense that a student who doesn't attend the extra classes is going to be left behind. Just last year a high official in the National Education Department made a strong public statement in opposition to the *pu-hsi-pan* system, but at the same time his own children were all attending *pu-hsi-pan*. When questioned about this he answered, "What else can I do? I oppose the *pu-hsi-pan* because it is bad, but what would happen to my children if they failed the examinations?"

Parents resent the *pu-hsi-pan* system, both for the long hours it requires of their children—children from Tapu who go into Taipei to the most prestigious *pu-hsi-pan* do not get home until after 11 P.M.—and for the extra expense. Many parents are convinced that teachers purposely fail to teach the children during school hours so they will have to join the teachers' evening tutorial classes. In 1959 the official rate set by the National Education Department was NT $10 per month per student, but it was common knowledge that the rate charged was NT $30–40. Parents of students who passed the entrance exams were expected to "express their gratitude" with a gift of several hundred dollars. According to a friend who taught in a Taipei school, the teachers give the principal a gift of NT $2,000 or more so he will assign them to the upper grades, the grades, that is, from which students are recruited for tutorials.

In 1969 compulsory education was extended from six years to nine years, thus ending the cramming for the competitive examinations to get into the "best" lower middle schools. During my most recent visit to Taiwan (1970), figures were released indicating that children had increased in height and weight over their age groups of five years previous. The newspapers implied that this was the direct result of the shorter hours children were required to spend over their books. Although I think improved nutrition, which is affecting all age groups, is more immediately relevant, there is something wrong with an educational system that requires its students to spend up to eleven hours a day in classrooms to get an education fitting them at best for work as clerks or secretaries. For students who pass the exams that will get them into one of Taiwan's colleges and who then aspire to go abroad for advanced training, the waste is even more depressing. Despite all the years they have had to put into their education, most students must learn to think after they leave the island. They have mastered all the facts made available to them, but independent or creative thinking has been discouraged whenever it cropped up.

In 1959 in Peihotien the iniquities of the *pu-hsi-pan* system had little relevance for girls. Only two were then in middle school, and I knew of only four others who had attended for at least one year. Most Peihotien parents are genuinely pleased to have literate daughters, but even young parents listen to the older generation's counsel against educating girls so highly that they are troublesome to match when it comes time for them to marry. For some of the older generation, it seems senseless for a girl who could be helping at home or even earning money in a factory to be in school getting an expensive education that will only benefit her future husband's family. One of our staff members tried to talk the strong-willed Ong Bou-kui into letting her scholarly granddaughter attend a teacher-training school. Our assistant pointed out, "It wouldn't cost you any fees, and when she graduates, she can teach and help you." Ong Bou-kui asked, "Isn't it true that a teacher can only earn NT $500 per month?" "Yes." Ong Bou-kui: "If she goes to Normal High School for three years, then she will be nineteen and ready to get married.

The school may not cost anything, but she won't bring home any money either. If she can earn NT $300 per month now, the family will have enough. The money she is using to study now is all borrowed. I have to return it little by little. It really isn't that I don't want her to study, but I don't have the money. If she was a boy, I would let her go on. It isn't that I am hard-hearted, but a son stays in your own family."

Many of the girls were painfully aware of the ambivalence of their families toward spending money on them and even when allowed to continue in school found the emotional strain more difficult than the education. A very mature six-teen-year-old told us the reasons she had quit school after the fifth grade (even though she had been first in her class every year but one): "My father's temper is very bad. That is one of the reasons I quit. The other reason was because my grand-mother was always complaining. 'What use is it for a girl to study? A girl should stay home and take care of the children.' At that time we were very poor, and every time I had to ask my father for money, he would scold me. Then, when I would go to school without the money, the teacher would scold me. I finally got mad and wouldn't go anymore. One good thing, though. My mother understood. Now whenever my younger sisters need money for school, she asks for it for them so they don't need to suffer from my father's temper."

What it is that motivates girls to do well in school is not easily analyzed. Parents withhold praise for good performance in the belief that the child will no longer try to do well. One mother told us, "I don't praise her when she brings home a good report because she would stop trying." Another said, "She is second in her class now. Last year she got 96 points on her examination and her father hit her four times to make 100 points." Even so, girls who do very well know their parents are impressed. Their teachers are less reticent about prais-ing them, holding them up before the class as an example to be copied. But what encourages the child of average ability who works hard to keep her place in the middle of the class hierarchy? School itself is no treat, but having to stay home when everyone else is in school would also be painful. "If she does poorly, I tell her that I won't let her continue to go to school because it embarrasses our family when she does poorly." A child who does very badly on an examination can expect a beating as well as humiliation before her peers. But probably the two factors that most strongly influence what might be mistaken as achievement motivation in girls are the school-encouraged trait of perseverance and their early training in obedience.

In rural Taiwan we found girls who had finished school but were not yet old enough to marry, i.e., teen-agers, the most difficult of all age categories to interview. It is far easier to get a shy six-year-old girl who has never before laid eyes on a huge, pale-eyed foreigner to tell you about her attitude toward her younger brother than it is to get a sixteen-year-old girl to tell you what time it is. They cover their extraordinary embarrassment with giggles if in a group or blank looks of total incomprehension if caught alone. Their problem seems to be one that was classic in the West before "teen-ager" became a separate status with its own mores, values, and accepted behavior patterns. They are neither children nor adults and are paralyzed by uncertainty when a new situation requires that they be one or the other.

An old lady told us that in the old days in Taiwan a girl was a child until she menstruated and as soon as possible after that she became a married woman. In modern Taiwan, probably as the result of improved nutrition, menarche comes to many girls while they are still in school, particularly now that compulsory education has been extended to nine years. Apparently some Taipei schools lecture about menstruation in girls' physical education classes and, in the most general of terms, its relationship to reproduction, but few country schools have taken on this responsibility. There is a puzzling ignorance on the part of prepubescent girls about the basic facts of menstruation. Our nineteen-year-old interpreter, who came from a family of ten children, insisted that the first she heard about menstruation was when a girl in her sixth-grade class started to menstruate at school and, convinced she was bleeding to death, became so hysterical it took several women teachers to calm her. The result was a very rudimentary lecture about menstruation for the rest of the upset girls. Village women told us much the same thing: they knew nothing about the subject until they began to menstruate, and even then their mothers only told them how to keep themselves clean and the ritual restrictions imposed on menstruating women.

By the time of her menarche there can be little doubt in a girl's mind that she and her sisters are not the equals of their brothers, and the new set of restrictions imposed on her as the result of her maturing body can only emphasize that point. She discovers that her body is a source of filth that can endanger others as well as herself. She may not enter a temple during her menses, for her unclean state would anger the gods, perhaps to the point of causing illness to strike her in revenge. A menstruating woman cannot attend the annual firewalking lest her presence cause the men who walk on the coals to burn their feet. Indeed, the purpose of the firewalking is often explained as "cleansing" the god of the defilement accumulated by contact with menstruating women. Such cleansing is necessary even if the contact amounts to nothing more than the god having been carried under a clothes pole hung with "the dirty cloths of a woman."

Most girls learn of the polluting potential of their bodies

even before they begin to menstruate. We saw a seven-year-old girl get a beating, at her grandfather's orders, because she was found playing an innocent game with her little brother that involved his passing between her legs. When we asked her grandmother what was wrong with their play, we found it was not the suspicion of sexuality that had incurred the grandfather's wrath, but simply that the crotch is the "dirty" part of a female, even an immature female, and therefore dangerous to baby brother. On another occasion we saw three girls gang up on a smaller boy, and while one held him down the others passed their legs over his head, taunting him with each pass that he would be stunted in size, a cripple, and so on. Unfortunately for them, these three little girls soon found that their newly discovered "power" was more of a handicap to its owners than a help.

When we talked to old ladies in Peihotien about "the old days," we were often told that women in the generation *before* theirs were secluded. The following is a typical story.

At that time a hired man who lived with a family would never even see the young women of the family. The only women he might see would be the really old ones. One of our relatives who used to live here had a daughter, and everyone knew he had a daughter, but no one had ever seen her. When there was a big flood and everyone was running for his life, her older brother wrapped her in a blanket and carried her out. Even then they wouldn't let anyone see her. Before, women didn't go out of the house unless something really bad happened. Buying food and everything was all done by the men. It wasn't like it is now, where the women take care of the guests and go into Tapu to buy things. The men who came to work for a family couldn't wander around the house like now. When they came in from the fields, they were supposed to go to their sleeping rooms and stay there. They couldn't go to the kitchen. They had a separate place to wash and if they needed water, it was the men from the family who brought it to them. The women only did the housework and cooked. When it was about time to eat, the women would put all the food on the table and then stay in their rooms until the men finished. It wasn't easy to get a look at a woman in those days.

One of our blunter informants in Peihotien snorted at this story and gave little credence to similar ones. She said that she had also heard tales of women being kept hidden "in the old days," but the "old days" were nearly always in the youth of the storyteller's grandmother. In her own youth (she was fifty-three in 1960), and as far as she could remember it was the same in her mother's descriptions, women were not as free to come and go outside their homes as now. Young women, married and unmarried, were expected to stay particularly close to home and to avoid any communication with members of the opposite sex. But at harvest time the men in farm families did not have time to do household chores for the bands of laborers who came up from the south to help with the huge job of cutting and threshing the rice. The chores were done by women as usual. It is true that it is easier "to get a look at a woman" now than it was, since women now do many of the errands in the market town, but this may be only because today it is safe to do so. A hundred years ago Taiwan was so threatened by bandit gangs, feuds between descent groups, and head-hunting aborigines that men did not travel any distance without armed companions either.

In 1959 there remained, however, a very definite reticence on the part of the senior generations to allow their unmarried daughters anything like the freedom of movement they allowed their sons. Factories were just beginning to have an influence on Peihotien. At that time there were forty unmarried girls living in the village who had finished their schooling and were potential factory employees. Tapu, the market town, and a nearby city both had a number of factories that employed young women. But Peihotien had its own little in-

97

dustry, a small factory that employed anywhere from four to twelve girls, depending on the owner's business luck. The pay was appreciably lower than that in "outside" jobs, but as parents were quick to point out, the girls did not have to buy uniforms or "good" clothes, could come home for lunch, and had no transportation costs. There were two further advantages: the only young man who worked in the factory was a cross-eyed, none-too-bright relative of the owner, and the location of the factory made it very convenient for mothers or siblings to drop in for a quick look around during the day. After a year or two in Peihotien's little factory, nearly every girl had a school friend who offered to "introduce" her to the manager of a factory "outside." Failing a friend to make such an introduction, few girls would go alone to apply for work at a strange factory. However, sometimes when the village factory laid off three or four girls at the same time, they would give each other the courage to make applications in Tapu's factories. Their parents were then faced with what was for many a painful decision. In 1959 the majority of the parents still could not bring themselves to let their daughters work outside the village. The parents of twelve of the forty unmarried girls had given in. Whenever the topic came up, the parents of two of the twelve were always quick to point out that their daughters were in the employ of some very close relatives. The wages the girls earned were a pittance, starting at NT $200 a month, but the quality of a girl's dowry and thus the ease of her first few years of marriage might depend on just this small addition to the family budget. For several families a daughter's job offer came just at the time the family was feeling the pinch of another child entering school or an unexpected medical expense.

In 1959 there were seven young women who made truly substantial contributions to their families' incomes. These were the girls who had been sent to work in brothels. One very bright, very attractive girl made between NT $2,500 and NT $3,500 a month, more than most young men of equal education could earn; another less intelligent and less attractive girl, who had borne one child and had had several abortions, had a guaranteed minimum salary of NT $1,000 plus a percentage of whatever gifts she received. Because of their occupation, these young women have quite different expectations from life. But as we shall see in Chapter 13 when we discuss in more detail the lives of village women who become prostitutes, even though the position they occupy in Peihotien's society is undeniably different from that of their peers, it is considerably more tolerable than it would be if they lived in an American small town.

By 1968 parental attitudes had apparently changed a great deal. In conversations with old friends from Peihotien, I learned that working in a factory after primary school is now almost as automatic for girls as going from the fourth grade to the fifth. The problem has become not so much a matter of convincing parents that it is safe, i.e., will not hinder a girl's chance for a respectable marriage, as of finding a good job. In the farmhouses I visited around Sanhsia, my impression was that the only young unmarried women who were at home either worked night shifts or were staying away from work because of illness. Literally hundreds of young women from the Sanhsia area climbed on the buses and trucks sent for them each morning to take them to the factories that now ring the southern edge of Taipei. Their wages are shockingly low, but unlike their sisters of twenty years ago, they can bring an income into the family without sacrificing any chance for a normal future. A worthless girl is no longer quite as worthless as she once was.

7

Engagement

What parents fear most for their daughters when they send them off to work in the new factories is that they will become entangled in a romance with a young man who would not be an appropriate mate. Except for their relatives, girls have very little experience in forming anything but the most superficial relationship with the opposite sex. The "problem" of co-educational schools in China is handled by strict segregation: boys sit on one side of the room and girls on the other. A boy is required to sit next to a girl as a form of punishment. Girls compete as a group with their male classmates for better grades, neater desks, and "quieter" rows. Boys are the enemy. Most girls are sexually mature by the time they go to work in factories, but their attitude toward boys is still the hostile one of childhood. Interaction consists primarily of the tossing of insults from a group of girls (and it is a rare thing to find a Taiwanese girl without at least two giggling companions) as they hurriedly pass a knot of boys. With age and experience the opposing camps learn to enjoy these exchanges and to pause in order to carry them further. To an outsider it seems highly unlikely that even an experienced rake could carry on a flirtation with a girl who is never separated from her two or three tittering girl friends, but oddly enough it is often these innocent girl friends, influenced by the saccharine sentimentality of Chinese movies, who bring on the disaster parents worry about.

A spark of interest between teen-agers, which would be quickly tested in America in conversations and a date or two, and then allowed to wane as other interests arose, is not so easily tested *or* abandoned in Taiwan. Any attraction between a boy and a girl becomes magnified if opposed—and all relationships not parentally sanctioned are opposed. Before even exchanging so much as a half-dozen words a young couple may find themselves romanticized by their friends as starcrossed lovers. Young friends eager to participate vicariously in the romance arrange a meeting between the two that cannot be casual because of the necessity for secrecy. As a result, the young couple find themselves committed to expressing to each other emotions they may not feel, anything less seeming inappropriate to the amount of effort that went into the meeting. Their well-meaning friends thus trap them into a relationship over which they have scarcely more control than if their parents had arranged it. In Peihotien in 1958 there were two recent and unhappy "love marriages" that had come to pass under these circumstances.

In the years between our first field trip and our return in 1968 I was told by American friends living in Taipei and Taiwanese students in American universities that dating had become permissible and young people considerably more independent. Although this certainly proved true of the college student population in contact with our American informants, the changes in the villages by 1968 were much less dramatic. There were a few more love marriages in Peihotien in 1968 than there had been in 1958 (apparently there have always been a few), but they were still not in the majority. Young people had a great deal more to say about who they would *not* marry, but they were not eager to assume the responsibility of choosing the person they *would* marry. The idea of doing something modern, something adventurous, is appealing to country girls, but it is the idea that is appealing, not the act. Love marriages are the stuff of daydreams, dreams that even the more naïve girls savor and forget. They have around them examples of some love marriages a few years old. What started out as simple attraction had no chance to mature before the couple found themselves pressured to formalize the relationship. As often as not, a few months after the wedding ceremonies the girls found that, like their mothers before them, they had married strangers—only they had chosen the strangers themselves. What is worse, by making the choice themselves they had in most cases sacrificed their families' support and caused most older people to question their reliability.

Although it is true that a married woman cannot expect financial support from her parents if the marriage they arrange for her is unsatisfactory, she can go to them for advice and use their home as a place to heal her wounds; and if she is truly mistreated, her family can be expected to exert all the social pressure at its command to remedy the situation. The girl who has chosen her own mate, often breaking harshly with her parents over the issue, has nowhere to go, a predicament that a resentful mother-in-law is sure to take full advantage of. As a middle-aged mother explained to us: "It's like I told you. If your parents arrange the marriage and something bad happens later, then you can come home and tell your parents about it. But if they didn't arrange it, then you won't dare do this. If you pick out your own, you might get along with him a little better, but then the other people have no responsibility for it. Like my daughter. I am very glad that everyone in that family likes her very much, or else I don't know how mad she would be. All she complains about now is that I made her marry too early so she didn't have a chance to play at all. If you let your parents arrange your marriage for you, your reputation will be better. People will say that you are a good girl because you allow your parents to decide all this for you."

A young man who comes home and announces that he wishes to marry a certain girl, or worse yet, *must* marry her and soon, creates problems that his parents will eventually charge to the account of his young wife. From his mother's point of view, the girl obviously is of a very independent nature, or she would not have trapped their son in the first place. How can such a girl ever become a good daughter-in-law, i.e., submissive, willing to take on the household drudgery and accept patiently her mother-in-law's ill-humored commands? She will be eager to divide the family and set up a separate home, depriving the parents of their son's love and labor. If she is from a family richer than theirs she will be unwilling or perhaps incapable of counting each penny as a good farmer's wife must. Her beauty attracted their son, but do slim hips indicate that she will have trouble bearing children and lacks the strength to help with the heavy chores? And will her family take advantage of their son's determination to demand a huge bride price?

In view of the risk the boy's family is required to take, his parents may demand a particularly large dowry. If, however, the girl is not pregnant but simply in love, her family can make use of the traditional means of negotiating an equitable balance between bride price and dowry. What her parents fear more is that their daughter has made a foolish choice. A woman who had just completed the arrangements for her older daughter's engagement and was already beginning to worry about a more troublesome younger daughter told us the main difference between marriages arranged by parents and those arranged by the children is that a girl will choose a man to marry whereas her parents will choose a family.

This may in fact be the reason why love marriages in rural Taiwan have not been noticeably more successful than those arranged solely at the discretion of the parents. No matter how a marriage is arranged, if the young man has not completely severed relations with his family—still a grave act on Taiwan—he must bring his bride home to his family to live. A clever girl may choose a handsome, intelligent, thoughtful young man as a husband, but she probably will not know that his mother is infamous for her control over him or for her cruelty to her other daughters-in-law, or that his father is a notorious drunkard who sells the doweries of his daughters-in-law, beats his wife, and keeps his sons on short rations.

If, as is more likely, the girl marries into a fairly normal family, she nonetheless has marital troubles. No matter how good a face the mother-in-law tries to put on it, she resents the girl for "stealing" her son. She had counted on selecting her son's wife herself—indeed had considered it her prerogative. From her point of view her son is hers, the only male she can ever claim, and now there is a competing claim. She must accept into the family of her creation a person who has challenged her authority once, and who will surely do so again. She is not going to be reticent about encouraging any differences that arise between the young husband and his wife. Although the husband's younger sisters may secretly admire their new sister-in-law's emancipated stand, they too resent her intrusion into their family, loyally reflecting their mother's attitude in any conflict. Peer group cohesiveness is still a phenomenon confined to the wealthier urban classes. Even the bride's father-in-law, who traditionally should be totally detached from her affairs, resents her as a symbol of his son's challenge to his authority.

Unless an outsider is told which couples made love marriages, he is not likely to distinguish them from other married couples in the village. They are not noticeably more intimate, they do not quarrel less, and the wives do not seem much happier. In other words, love marriages simply do not provide a very attractive example for the young unmarried men and women in the village. In view of such mediocre results and the immense strain required to achieve a love marriage, it is not surprising that the majority of the girls from rural communities are still content to have their parents take the responsibility for arranging their futures.

At about the same time that the values of sentimental movies and romantic peers are exerting pressures toward emotional involvements, mother-daughter relations also begin to take on a different character. Mothers are usually only amused by the first few inquiries go-betweens make about their daughters, but they do begin to look at the girls in a new way, noticing perhaps for the first time a bit of themselves in the girls' gestures and seeing the movements of a young woman emerging from the gawky walk of adolescence. A girl's interest in acquiring the trappings of adulthood involves her in conversations with her mother that engage the mother's interests as an individual and not just as a mother. A new intimacy develops between them, and the mother's confidences about her own life may have a very sobering effect on her daughter. All the values of the girl's society tell her that it is her family on which she can depend and outsiders who are the source of danger. If her peers have been encouraging her in a romantic fantasy, conversations with her mother may put the world back into perspective, the conservative perspective of a long tradition.

Traditional Taiwanese engagement and wedding ritual is so richly colorful that the foreign observer is often tempted to dwell on the ceremonies to the detriment of the topics that more closely concern the Taiwanese. The "social research" and negotiation that precede a conventional engagement are of much more interest to the Taiwanese observer. The ceremony simply signifies their successful completion. In Taiwanese terms a wedding ceremony is not an act by which two people are united as a married couple, but an announcement to the ancestors and to the numerous friends and relatives invited to feast that the family has taken a daughter-in-law, the first step to extending itself yet another generation.

Except in the case of an uxorilocal marriage (see Chapter 12), the family of a marriageable girl does not take the initiative in finding a suitable husband for her. At least it does not admit to doing so. Since serving as a go-between is considered a good thing (a proverb states that to get into heaven everyone must arrange at least one marriage in his life) and since there seems to be a universal penchant in the human race for exchanging information about the lives of one's neighbors, the availability of a young woman for marriage is not likely to be overlooked. Parents who for some reason are anxious to marry their daughter early can make this known without actively searching for a husband for her. The prospective groom's family must appoint the go-between (usually a woman), and a friend who happens to know a young woman meeting all of the family's requirements may quite naturally become the go-between. Sometimes, for one reason or another, a friend who suggests a likely candidate cannot serve as the go-between. In that case the groom's family selects a go-between solely for her talents and loyalty rather than because she "knows a girl." This is probably the only situation in which the groom's family can be entirely certain that *it* selected the go-between. A suitable go-between is mature, patient, capable of stating a position strongly and withdrawing from it graciously, a good observer, and well-versed in local custom. She must come from a local family, because only families who have been neighbors for several generations can be trusted, and because variation in custom from even one valley to the next is considerable.

Engagement

In the villages, the initial discussion from which a marriage stems probably occurs between two women washing clothes on the riverbank or cleaning vegetables next to the neighborhood well. Sometimes it comes as a sudden inspiration; other times it is carefully staged as a sudden inspiration. Mothers with daughters of marriageable age become very self-conscious about such "casual" suggestions. If the suggestion was truly unstaged, the girl's family may in effect have chosen the go-between. It is clearly bad form as well as bad tactics for a would-be go-between to let the boy's family know that she has already raised the topic with the girl's family, an act that might cast doubt on her loyalties to the boy's family. The deceiving go-between is the subject of many stories exchanged in women's gossip sessions. One of my favorites is of the go-between who arranged a marriage between a young man with a twisted leg and a very ugly girl. The boy and his family were to look the girl over by walking past her house when she was strolling in the yard, giving her and her family a similar opportunity. For the occasion, the boy's family replaced him with his brother, and the girl stayed hidden indoors while her sister promenaded. After the "viewing," the go-between told each family, "Now you have seen for yourselves. If the boy turns out crippled or the girl ugly, don't blame me."

Obviously these stories are more for fun than for instruction. Rarely is a family so bereft of kin and friends that it cannot get several independent opinions of a family proposed by a go-between. There is a general feeling that brides should not come from the same village as their husbands, but there is also a strong tendency for families to go again and again to a particular area to choose their brides and adopted daughters. Women return to their natal homes at least once a year and usually more often. These visits are naturally filled with conversations about who is looking for a wife and what girl is ready to marry. Secrets are hard to keep in rural communities; consequently, a family's relative wealth (and dowry potential) and the disposition of its members are common knowledge to those who live nearby. This information travels by means of the women who have married out, as does information about the people in the villages they have married into. The absence of such a network of information sources is one of the reasons concerned mothers find love marriages so difficult. They may be at a loss to judge the respectability and reputation of either the family or the individual because they do not know his neighbors or anyone who does.

The parents of a young man are less concerned about the girl's family than the girl's family is concerned about them, but they do have some criteria. "Matching doors" is important. Rich girls make poor wives for farmers. They do not know how to work, they do not know the value of money, they are likely to be independent, and they are likely to talk a great deal about how well off they were before they married. Even if a wealthy girl turns out to be a good wife and a good daughter-in-law, there is still a problem, for her family must be entertained on various occasions, and this can be both expensive and embarrassing. Yet a daughter-in-law with poor relatives also presents problems. They will frequently be asking for loans, or tempting their daughter's husband to join a loan association they have organized or some foolhardy business venture.

If the family under consideration is acceptable, attention turns to the girl's personal attributes. Every family wishes its son to marry an attractive (but not beautiful), healthy, strong, submissive, sweet-natured, modest young woman with a reputation unsullied by rumor. Choosing a daughter-in-law is a serious business for a Taiwanese family. Finding someone that will make the young man happy must remain a secondary issue, no matter how important it may seem to him. Chinese weddings are ruinously expensive, and most rural families can barely afford one per son. If the girl dies, the money is wasted. If she cannot endure the hardships of farm life or the harshness of her mother-in-law's regime and runs away, she wastes the family's money and injures its reputation. It will be harder to find another wife with all the rumors the first wife left behind. The most feared of all fates is that the bride proves to be barren. Then, the family feels intensely the burden of the ancestors, as well as anxieties about its own future, in old age and after death. Several of the brides who married into Peihotien during our years there were quite obviously pregnant, and their mothers-in-law were just as obviously pleased. If the bride passes all other tests but turns out to have a horrid nature, the family must resign itself to a lifetime of acrimony. Since it is the young man's mother who will suffer first and perhaps most from her daughter-in-law's personality, it is not surprising that she makes every effort to pick up warnings from gossip, from fortunetellers, and from omens.

The parents of any young woman who rates well on most of these criteria for the perfect daughter-in-law will get more and more frequent inquiries about their plans for her after she enters her seventeenth or eighteenth year. There are numerous ways in which a mother who would like to keep her daughter home a bit longer can appear to give serious consideration to each match suggested and to discover perfectly acceptable reasons for rejecting them one after another. But if she truly has her daughter's best interests at heart, she must use caution lest she cast out the marriage "recorded in Heaven." A go-between may attempt to arouse a fond mother's interest with a detailed description of the socioeconomic status of the prospective groom's family, but the mother's questions are more likely to show her interest in the structure of the family. Marriage to a firstborn son with several younger brothers means not only a lot of hard work, but also life in a family whose financial resources are beginning a period of intense strain as wives are brought in for the other sons. It also means having a mother-in-law who is as yet untested in that role. If the woman should turn out to be a difficult personality, the wife of the firstborn son will suffer the most from her bad nature, since there is a presumption that the firstborn son will be the one to stay with the elderly parents in the event the family is divided.

When a go-between finally suggests a marriage that interests a young woman's parents enough to alert their friends and relatives to gather information for them, the mother will want to know everything that can be discovered about the personalities and habits of the family members—information that a go-between is likely to be less than honest about. A young man will not be rejected simply because he has visited wineshops and brothels with his friends, but if he is reputed to be a regular customer, the problem requires more consideration. Occasional gambling is also overlooked, but again, if the young man is rumored to gamble frequently or to have large losses, he is a risky mate. Similar information about his father or any other male in the family makes the marriage equally risky. While the girl's mother is making her inquiries, her father researches the family's financial stability, its prospects, and the earning potential of the young man and his brothers, and if the relative status of the family warrants, he attempts to discover if there is any hidden motive in its interest in an alliance with his family. All the while, of course, he is evaluating what advantage such an alliance may have for his family in the years to come. He may well be as concerned about his daughter's comfort as his wife is, but his obligations are to his ancestors and their descendants. In practice, this often allows for more consideration of a daughter's personal desires than of a son's. In contracting the marriage of a son, the interests of the family are foremost; but in contracting the marriage of a daughter, as long as the family is not ill-served, her welfare can be foremost. The family in fact would be ill-served if for greed alone it gave its daughter to the family that offered the highest bride price. The case would provide gossip for the village for years to come.

Many Taiwanese girls grow up as their father's favorite—he brings them special treats, tolerates their disobedience, chuckles at an insolence for which he would have beaten his sons, and protects them from the often-deserved punishments threatened by their mothers. The relationship is a refuge of affection for the man who must be a stern disciplinarian with his sons and is often distant in his interaction with his wife. Perhaps because such a relationship is not formalized in Chinese culture—is in fact against many of the culture's precepts—it rarely matures beyond a superficial adult-child level. Before the girl is old enough to develop the understanding of her father's problems necessary for any depth in their relations, she begins to identify with her mother and to discover their shared interests. Her father then becomes less her protector (an unnecessary role now, since it was from her mother's discipline that he was protecting her) and more her mother's oppressor. The authoritarian image required of a man in his public relations with his wife is often pure sham, and a woman who respects and appreciates her husband will attempt to convey this to her daughter. For some girls this knowledge may provide only further evidence of their mother's martyrdom. Obviously, a woman who resents her husband will take this opportunity to repay him by increasing the growing estrangement between him and his favorite daughter.

No matter how well a man gets on with his wife, the imminent engagement of a favorite daughter must be a difficult period in his life. As the go-betweens make inquiries about his daughter and the negotiations for her marriage begin, he is torn between his emotional attachment to the girl and the obligation of doing what is best for his descent line. Whereas his wife can immediately express her dislike of a proposed match and refuse to even consider a marriage into the family of a wealthy local businessman whose wife is known to torment her daughters-in-law, he must weigh the advantages of having an affinal tie with such a family—some day his sons or grandsons may benefit considerably from such a contact. The father may be just as eager as the mother to reject the match and for precisely the same reasons, but for the benefit of his relatives and neighbors, who will evaluate his decisions as a family manager and perhaps even the general moral fiber of his family, he must first discover a way to discount the advantages to his family of such a union. Unless his daughter is truly his confidante, his attitude toward her marriage must seem callous. Fathers, because they are men, must live within the rules; mothers need only decide what is best for their daughter.

The distinction between the traditional methods of selecting a mate for a son and his "falling in love" and choosing his own wife is beginning to blur in rural Taiwan and may soon be indistinguishable. Whether this will mean the end of love marriages or the end of traditional marriages is a matter of semantics. A young man may be attracted by the behavior (or eyebrows) of a girl he sees at work every day but in his shyness have done nothing about it. Or he may have become well acquainted with the girl without confiding in his family. When his parents begin to speak insistently about his marriage, he is likely to mention this girl. Unless his parents have another very serious prospect in mind, they ask a go-between to make inquiries about the young lady. Since parents and grandparents are usually ready for the young men to marry considerably sooner than they themselves are, a family will probably be prepared to lay before a son several other choices. He is shown pictures, given descriptions, and encouraged to catch a glimpse of any of the girls that interest the parents. He may find the girl who originally caught his fancy less interesting than one of those on his mother's list. Or he may simply play a waiting game until the family's choice and his own coincide.

When the go-between feels that both families know enough about each other to have rejected the match if they had no serious interest in it, she will urge a formal meeting. Ten years ago, it was just that: the boy and his mother and perhaps a relative or two accompanied by the go-between arrived at an appointed hour and were served tea by the girl, bolstered by her relatives. Both young people were rigid with embarrassment and often could not even bring themselves to look at each other. They gained little from a meeting that was ostensibly for their benefit, but then, fifty years ago no consideration of their opinions was offered at all. One mother who had pressured her son into several of these affairs told us that she had given up and was urging him to go find his own wife. "Every time I find a girl for him to look at now he refuses to go. He says the girl's family just waits to look him over as though he was a pig for sale. He told me last week, 'I don't care if she is blind or without legs. If she is willing, that's fine. If she isn't willing, then that's fine too. But I won't go to look at her.' "

Modern innovations on "the meeting" change the setting to respectable sweetshops in Taipei with only the go-between and the two mothers, who are expected to make conversation among themselves and allow the couple to talk alone. Obviously, many country people feel very uncomfortable in such a setting, a trip to Taipei in itself being quite an experience. The most common initial meeting remains the home visit, but the events that follow are nowadays often as individual as the people involved. One of the young people may simply refuse the match, in which case the go-between tells the other family that her clients have decided not to marry just now or gives some other face-saving fabrication. But if there is no outright refusal, the negotiations continue between the families, ultimately resulting in a marriage between the couple, who may not lay eyes on each other again until the day of the wedding. In some cases, further meetings may be arranged, even to the point of the two meeting alone and attending a movie without chaperones. Where once all contact between two families considering a marriage was controlled by a go-between, many young people now complicate the negotiations by initiating another level of interaction. It is here that the distinction between the love marriage and the arranged marriage begins to fail. In the following conversation between a village woman whose son was just about to be engaged and her relative whose daughter was being much visited by go-betweens, the complications of the "arranged love marriage" are touched on, displaying the antagonism of a future mother-in-law who was very much in favor of the match originally.

Mui-hiong: "The engagement will be on the nineteenth. I really don't like the girl, but my son wants her, so . . . You know he is already twenty-six, and when someone asks me how old he is, I'm embarrassed [because he was not married yet]. At first I was going to get him a wife when he was twenty-three, but then we built the new house and had to wait for a while [a matter of money]. Mainly it was my son's idea because he wanted to wait until the new house was done." Ai-gioq: "Twenty-six isn't so old nowadays. Most of the people suggested for my girl are nearly thirty, so how can you be embarrassed?" Mui-hiong: "Well, I am, but then the girl is already twenty-two. The reason this marriage is coming about is because the people from my parents' home came all the time to talk about it. Really, I wasn't too interested in it because there were so many other possibilities. The girl isn't very pretty—quite large and coarse. I don't like that type. I like small, fine-boned girls like your daughter. It's a shame that marriage couldn't have been arranged" [they were relatives of the same surname]. Ai-gioq: "Oh, Mui-hiong, that is not what is important. When you choose a daughter-in-law you should just be sure that she has the three degrees of obedience [to her parents, to her husband, and to her son] and the four feminine virtues [proper behavior, demeanor, speech, and employment]. Prettiness is not useful. When they come to talk about my daughter I don't want to hear how handsome the boy is or how much they offer for a bride price, as long as he is a good boy and his family is good." Mui-hiong: "Of course you are right. The go-between keeps telling me that this girl is very good and very willing to work. She says if we don't marry her, we will regret it forever. Maybe she is right. But you know, after this girl met my son and found out where he worked, she often went there to 'block the road' [to wait for him after work]. Then they began to act like it was a love match, and I just had to go ahead with it. But I am angry with them. Each time the go-between comes the family wants something more. At first they said the number of cakes was up to us, and they wanted only 320 unboxed cakes [to announce the engagement to friends], but now they want 180 boxed cakes besides. The cakes alone will cost NT $4,000 [U.S. $100]. Who wouldn't be mad? Besides this, they want a gold necklace and two gold bracelets. They won't take the *tua tia:*, they only want the *siou tia:*.* Really, it is only because my son wants her that we are willing to go so high. They are not a family with a great deal of face. Won't they be embarrassed to take that much cake? Her father is only a workman in the winery [Mui-hiong's husband outranked him a little] and I don't think her dowry will amount to much." Ai-gioq:

---

* *Tua tia:* means "large betrothal money" and *siou tia:* "small betrothal money." These gifts to the bride's family are commonly referred to in the literature as bride price. They are discussed in detail on pages 119–20.

"Oh well, these things don't really matter. What is important is if the girl is good.* Here my daughter is already twenty-three years old, and we haven't found anyone for her to marry yet." [It was commonly said in the village that if Thi:-kong, the highest god, offered to marry Ai-gioq's daughter, Ai-gioq would still find something wrong with the match.] Mui-hiong: "That is just because her destined time hasn't come about yet. You don't need to worry. When the time arrives it will be all right. You know, my real brother's wife's neighbors have a very nice family. [Mui-hiong was adopted out as a child but still maintains relations with her natal family.] They own their own coal mine. After I finish with my son's engagement, I'll go talk to them. Their boy is very nice looking, and if a marriage was arranged there, it would be very 'free.' Their eldest son and his wife live in a separate house and have their own share in the mine. This would be a good marriage for your daughter. She is much too delicate to marry into the country." Ai-gioq: "Well, if you think it might be good . . . I don't care about the bride price as long as the boy can make a good living for her and doesn't live too far away. There have been so many go-betweens. . . . The last one was my step-mother's real brother's wife. She talked a long time about a marriage. They really like my girl. I finally went and asked the gods, and they said it wasn't too good, so I wasn't very willing. Later the family sent someone again, and that same day someone stepped on one of my chickens and killed it. Then I really didn't approve of the match. I didn't actually make a request of the gods, but I think that was a sign from them." Mui-hiong: "There is another family I know of right in Tapu. They have quite a bit of money and a servant who

* Although the rest of this conversation is off the topic of "arranged love marriages," I include it because it is a good example of the kind of conversation that often leads to a marriage.

116

does all the housework. They asked me to look for a girl for them. Maybe they would be a good match."

If the young people do not turn down the match after their formal introduction, and the two families find nothing prejudicial about each other, the next official step is "exchanging the eight characters." The year, month, day, and hour of birth of the boy and the girl are written on red cards and exchanged. Each family places the card it received from the other family on its ancestral altar for three days to obtain the opinion of the family's ancestors and any gods who might be on the altar. A negative opinion is expressed by the death of a domestic animal, a family quarrel, an illness, something being broken or lost, or any other minor or major domestic tragedy. If either family decides for any reason that it does not wish to continue negotiations, a dropped rice bowl provides a simple solution that cannot offend anyone. There are still families who take such portents very seriously, keeping a complete record of any unusual events during this period, carefully questioning their meaning with the help of a fortuneteller, the priest in the temple, and inquiries of the gods on their domestic altar. If nothing untoward has happened at the end of three days, the girl's family takes both sets of eight characters to a fortuneteller to discover from his calculations how well suited the couple are to each other. Knowledgeable and cautious families have corrected in so far as possible any "errors" of birth that might make it difficult for their daughter to marry, changing the time or date to a more agreeable combination. But there is little they can do about a girl born in the Year of the Tiger, which makes her dangerous to people in particular ritual states, or in, say, the "broken months" (the third, sixth, and ninth), which indicate that her carelessness and clumsiness will bring endless small misfortunes to those around her. Moreover, even a family that has managed to register its daughter's birth on a good day in a good month at a good hour may find that her characters combine badly with the boy's, or that if she marries in this, her nineteenth (or whichever), year, she will bring on bad luck. One young woman we knew in Peihotien idly visited a fortuneteller only to be told that because she was so pretty she must either marry before she reached nineteen or "pay her flower debt" by working as a prostitute for a set number of years. Needless to say, her mother found this reading entirely unacceptable (the girl was aproaching her twenty-first birthday) and hurried her off to a more agreeable fortuneteller, who discovered alternative ways of "paying the flower debt."

Although there are a number of acceptable reasons why a potential match may be dropped up to and even after the eight characters have been exchanged, once the characters are "approved" and returned it becomes difficult for either party to withdraw gracefully. On one level this can be explained by pointing out that the purpose of the investigation of the eight characters is to discover if the proposed match is the one "recorded in Heaven" for the couple; if the characters indicate it is, there should be no question of cancellation. On a more mundane level, the approval and return of the eight characters indicate that the match is agreed on, and only outrageous demands or the discovery of grave problems can justify a withdrawal. In other words, from this point on, if the engagement is called off one side or the other must be blamed. Straightforward negotiations about the size of the bride price, the number of engagement cakes required, the quality and content of the dowry, and the various gifts to be exchanged will not begin until after the commitment of the eight characters. However, few go-betweens would risk their own reputation or that of the family they represent by not having a clear understanding with both parties about the range within which they will negotiate. It is at this point that the difficulties between the traditional approach to marriage and the modern involvement of the young people begin to surface. In the past a simple change of mind was not an adequate explanation, since marriages were not a matter of inclination but negotiated alliances between two families. When a lack of inclination calls off a nearly concluded engagement, the older generation in the society still looks to the traditional explanations for the cause.

It is the painful period of serious economic negotiation between the acceptance of the eight characters and the engagement ceremony that gives rise to (and often the truth to) the well-known proverb "Marriage makes kinsmen of bitter enemies." Even a very parsimonious family spends half a year's income acquiring a bride, and every dollar spent is carefully accounted for. No family expects its go-between to negotiate a major saving in money, for a bride who comes as a bargain will be presumed flawed by the neighbors. But no family wants to spend any more than is absolutely necessary for the face it feels appropriate to its situation in life. Unfortunately, in this case the family is negotiating with someone else's face. There are two sums of money offered to the bride's family, the *tua tia:* (large bride price) and the *siou tia:* (small bride price). The bride's family may refuse the *tua tia:*, but even wealthy families usually accept a token *siou tia:*. The go-between usually establishes which the bride's family will take before the eight characters are accepted. Although there is a range in the amount of the *siou tia:* and the *tua tia:* that is considered conventional for the area and social class of the families, a family that has agreed to take the *siou tia:* and then finds the groom's family beginning negotiations at the very lowest amount may insist on the *tua tia:*. The problem is not simply one of dollars and cents. The bride's position in her new family and village is affected by the display of dowry that precedes her entry. Although her father may gain face by accepting only the *siou tia:*, and a small *siou tia:* at that, if he cannot then provide out of his own pocket a thoroughly respectable dowry for her, he has made her life more difficult than necessary and, in so doing, has lost face where he hoped to gain. In Peihotien a young woman who had already borne two children was still suffering from her father's lack of finesse. He had returned all the *tua tia:*, had accepted the minimum *siou tia:*, and then had been unable to provide his daughter with more than a few items of clothing in the way of a dowry. To this day when her mother-in-law gets angry with her, she makes caustic comments about brides who arrive empty-handed.

The engagement of a young relative of the family with whom we lived in Peihotien provides an excellent example of how an incompetent go-between can make the first taste of marriage bitter. Miss Lim, the only daughter of a prosperous farm family with several sons, was twenty-three before her mother found a family that met all her qualifications for a future for her favorite child. The go-between, the mother's younger sister, had obvious loyalties to the family. However, the go-between was apparently too thoroughly convinced that this marriage was "recorded in Heaven." When the *siou tia:* was presented on the day of the engagement, it contained only NT $2,200, a sum considered unusually low. In an interview several days later, Miss Lim told us, "While we were still talking about the marriage we told the go-between that we wanted NT $6,200 at least for the *siou tia:*. She just said not to worry because this family understood about social relationships, and there would be no problem. We also had her tell the boy's family not to send a lot of gifts for the engagement. The boy's family told us, 'When we come it is a matter of our face, and when you go it is a matter of your face.' When I opened that envelope and saw how small the *siou tia:* was, I had to sit down I was so surprised and so angry. They just thought about their own face and paid no attention to ours." Mrs. Lim, the mother, commented, "When they give such a small *siou tia:* you can't say that this doesn't concern their face too. My oldest son says we do not need to say anything because they have lost more face than we have, and it would only be embarrassing to say anything to them." Miss Lim responded, "Yes, don't say anything about it! Don't say anything about it! Just let everyone talk about us!" Her mother turned to her and said, "What can you say to them? What good would it do now to say anything?" Miss Lim, who was really very angry, said, "All right, it's useless. It's useless. Let's just forget the whole thing [i.e., call off the marriage]." Her mother, quite startled, said, "You are talking like a crazy person. How can you say that?" Miss Lim, after calming down, went on to say, "Yesterday that boy [her future husband] came here, and I thanked him and said, 'You let me break a record in this village giving me so much money for the *siou tia:*!' I was going to say something more, but my mother came out and told me to be quiet because it wasn't his fault. And she is probably right. It is just that his mother isn't willing to let go of any money.... One of my [male] relatives is getting engaged soon, and the girl's family wants his family to give NT $6,200 for the *siou tia:*, let them take half of the *tua tia:*, and pay for all the furniture besides. When his family heard about my *siou tia:*, they went running back to the girl's family and told them they would have to pay for the furniture themselves. In this village the smallest *siou tia:* is NT $6,200. I have never even heard anyone say NT $2,200." (According to other informants, NT $3,200 was the smallest respectable amount in 1960.)

For all its careful planning, this Lim family chose for its daughter a family that was determined to get the most face for the least money. On the day of the engagement the groom's family is expected to leave an *ang pau* (a red gift envelope containing money) to pay for the engagement feast provided by the girl's family. The price of a table of guests is standard and therefore the item is rarely negotiated. This family left an *ang pau* containing NT $600 rather than the expected $800 per table. The Lims' retaliation was considered exquisitely appropriate by the more sophisticated villagers. At this point in the engagement procedure the groom's family is required to send "the twelve gifts," made up of pairs of items, including canned delicacies and such fresh foods as two fish, two ducks, two chickens, and the like. Although the bride's family should not accept all of these gifts, it must make a selection from among them; to return all of them, or even the majority of them would cost the groom's family face, because it would indicate that the gifts were unacceptable. The Lims took advantage of this custom to show their displeasure, returning almost all of the gifts, but with such a show of politeness that the groom's family was forced to present the gifts a second time. By this time it was late in the day, and the fresh meat was ripening in the hot summer weather, so the Lims had everything deposited in the Tapu ice house. They then made their position abundantly clear by returning the whole lot to Taipei the following day. With the utmost courtesy, they had made their irritation public. They also, to the amusement of their neighbors, cost the tight-fisted family of their daughter's future husband a sizable sum of money; not only did the spoiled meat have to be paid for, but the canned goods, which are normally rented from a "marriage shop," required two days' rental fees rather than one. The Lims' revenge would be complete on the day the dowry was delivered, assuming of course that the display it made was as dazzling as they planned.

Another expense for the groom's family that is often the subject of hostile negotiation is the gift of gold jewelry to the bride. Although these are personal gifts that return with the bride (and in this sense do not represent wealth lost to the groom's family), the bride's family knows that its gold and its social standing will be weighed on the same scale. In poor families this may be the only personal wealth a bride has to help her in an emergency. The minimum requirement consists of a gold bracelet, a gold necklace, and a gold ring. In earlier times golden hair ornaments were important items on the jewelry list. Obviously the wealthier the family the more elaborate the gift of gold, but quite often in farm families the family that insists on two gold rings will get two thin rings instead of one thick one.

Two types of cakes are sent out by the bride's family to announce her engagement: large unboxed cakes to friends, relatives, and neighbors, and boxed cakes (six in a box) to closer relatives, high-status acquaintances, and other people the family hopes to impress or obligate. The unboxed cake is simply an announcement, and nothing further is required, but the boxed cakes presume a wedding gift in return. Often friends of the bride, expecting only unboxed cakes, will request the other kind, a way of saying they intend to send the bride a gift. Although it is not a strict rule, friends usually send personal gifts, such as clothing, and relatives gifts of money. In 1968 in Sanhsia, unboxed cakes cost from NT $12 to NT $14, and boxed cakes cost from NT $22 to NT $26; in Taipei unboxed cakes cost from NT $17 to NT $19 and boxed cakes from NT $25 to NT $35. In recent years brides who work in factories feel required to present many of their friends at work with cakes. This can be expensive. For example, the engagement cakes required by the Miss Lim mentioned above, a girl who had never worked outside her home, cost nearly U.S. $200, and the family felt that it had been quite conservative. Since it is the groom's family that must pay for the cakes, this becomes another potentially disruptive subject for negotiation.

Although the bride's family is expected to give a complete

outfit of clothing to the groom on the day of the engagement, including a length of material to be tailored into a suit, this apparently is not a negotiable item. The bride's family will send the best it can afford. The dowry is the major expenditure over which the girl's family will worry, and with good reason. It precedes the bride to her new home three days before the wedding, carried on as many carts as possible over as long a route as is practicable. Wearing apparel, linens, fabric to make into clothing, and other goods are separately laid on trays in such a way as to make them appear thick and numerous. Even gifts of money are carefully pinned bill by bill on trays, which are then fastened to carts, one to a cart. Furniture is carried by the same method, with less attention paid to whether it gets scratched or dented than to whether each piece is given full view. Since it is usually the groom's family that must pay for the carts, the situation is again one in which one family is negotiating to save money at the cost of the other's face. Just how important the face value of the dowry is can be seen in the groups of neighbors that congregate when the dowry caravan arrives. Unlike Americans who hide behind curtains as they evaluate the quantity and quality of their new neighbors' furniture coming off the moving van, Chinese quite frankly tote up the number of carts and the approximate worth of each cart, and within a few minutes can give an accurate estimate of the amount spent on the dowry. The items of furniture to be included in the dowry are nearly always agreed on at the same time as the bride price is settled and therefore are known to most of the community before they arrive, but the clothing and personal items, and the luxury items, such as radios, cameras, and sewing machines, often come as a carefully planned surprise. It is for these that girls work overtime at the factories and mothers surreptitiously trim the food budget.

When the negotiations are nearly complete, the eight characters are again submitted to a fortuneteller or other specialist to calculate a date that is "fortunate" for both parties. This is, incidentally, another reason why girls born in the Year of the Tiger or on other "bad" dates are such a nuisance. Not only are they in some cases a ritual danger to others, they also have so few "good" days that it is difficult to find a day on which they can be safely engaged, married, or even buried. I suspect that the go-between often uses the setting of the date for the engagement ceremony as a ploy to accelerate lagging negotiations and soften up firm positions taken by either or both sides.

On the day of his engagement, the bridegroom goes about his work as usual. His parents, the go-between, and some relatives or family friends, making up a party of at least six (the word four has the same sound as the word for death and is therefore to be avoided), depart in the morning for the bride's house, accompanied by gifts and the engagement cakes. On arrival they are served sweet tea by the bride (for which they drop on the tray the ubiquitous *ang pau*). After she has left the room, the go-between formally asks both parties if they agree on the match, and receiving the expected affirmative answer, the girl is again summoned. She is seated by the go-between on a stool, facing the door of her father's house with her back to his ancestral altar. The symbolism is clear. The central act of the engagement, that is, the point after which the girl is irrevocably engaged, is both symbolically and tangibly the beginning of the struggle between mother-in-law and daughter-in-law. The mother-in-law attempts to place a gold ring on her daughter-in-law's finger, and the girl attempts to prevent her from getting it over her middle knuckle. If the girl fails, she will be dominated by her mother-in-law all her life. The more sophisticated village women are a bit embarrassed by this struggle, but it apparently has too much emotional significance to be abandoned. A part of the struggle used to include the older woman's desire to get a close look at the palm of the girl's hand before finalizing the engagement. If the future mother-in-law found a strong line crossing the girl's palm, she might insist that the marriage plans be abandoned. Such a line indicates that the young woman's fate is a threat to her future husband, and a mother-in-law who already sees the young woman as a threat to her own peace of mind will reject the engagement to protect her son. A Sanhsia man (who had made a love marriage) lost his jewelry store by a stroke of bad luck, after which his marriage ended in divorce. He told us with much chagrin that his mother had begged him not to marry the girl because of the line on her hand and now told him that he was lucky to get out of the marriage with his life.

In the past the engagement ceremony had to be completed before noon, or the marriage was fated for divorce. It is still commonly a morning ceremony, but not necessarily. The conclusion is marked, as are all Chinese events, by a feast for which the groom's family is expected to leave yet another *ang pau*. Thereupon the groom's family departs, carrying off the gifts it has received. Before the engagement cakes the boy's family brought are distributed to friends and relatives, they are spread in front of the family altar to announce to the ancestors that a girl is marrying out. Six of the cakes are specially marked with the character called double happiness and are not placed before the altar. They are sent to the groom's family, which uses them to inform his ancestors of the upcoming marriage. Another small group of cakes is set aside for the bride to eat. If she ate those offered to her father's ancestors, she would not be able to thrive on the food in her husband's house.

Even today in modern Taiwan a young couple who have been formally betrothed are as good as married. The elaborate expenditure of time, money, and energy is evidence of the seriousness with which the event is taken. To turn back at this point would be a social and economic disaster. Should one of the engaged pair ask to be excused because of a change of heart, both families would apply strong pressures to prevent it. The financial loss would be large on both sides, but it would be most costly to the family of the party who wished to renege, for it would have to pay damages in order to repair the other's face. Few young people in rural Taiwan would care to bear that burden of guilt.

8

Marriage

A very poor family tries to save money by holding a marriage a few days or even a few hours after the engagement. New shoes are still new shoes three days later, but not a year later, and one feast is cheaper than two. There are, to be sure, reasons aside from economy for telescoping the engagement and marriage ceremonies: a pregnant bride, a social solution for girls who marry mainlanders without families, couples who are marrying against their parents' will. Unless a young man has parents available to go to the girl's home, a traditional Taiwanese wedding is impossible; unless a girl has parents who are willing to engage her to the family of the man she has chosen, a traditional Taiwanese engagement is equally impossible. The absence of the engagement ceremony is less apparent when some variant of it is performed on the same day as the wedding. A death in the family is another circumstance under which a wedding might be set ahead. For reasons not entirely clear to me, a couple must marry within three months after a death in either family or wait a full year.

Ideally, about a year should elapse between an engagement and the marriage. In the past this was the minimum amount of time in which the bride and her female relatives could complete the various sewing projects essential to the dowry. In modern Taiwan many of the hand-worked items have been dropped from dowries, but for most families a year is still needed to accumulate the money to purchase dowry items. A couple whose wedding I attended in Sanhsia were not young when they finally became engaged and they delayed their marriage for two years because the young woman had a particularly well-paid job in a factory and the groom wanted to expand the family business before he took on the expense of a wedding. Aside from the economic advantages, the fact that the bride was the only daughter and youngest child of a woman who had four sons played no small part in the delay. The bride and her mother were clearly very close and reluctant to part.

The groom's family seldom has any desire to delay the wedding once it has the money to proceed. The exception is those families whose sons have not yet served their term in the military. Farm families nowadays do not wish to take responsibility for a young woman who is not really a member of the family and yet capable of bringing disgrace to it. The explanation we were given by mothers-in-law who seemed quite capable of managing their daughters-in-law under any other circumstances is that once young women have had sexual relations they are likely to become licentious if they do not have their husbands around to satisfy them. This notion seems particularly absurd in view of the very negative attitude most married women have toward their own sex life. I think the family's reluctance to take responsibility for a son's bride in his absence represents a new uncertainty about relationships within the family, a recognition (though not necessarily an acceptance) of a new emphasis on the husband-wife relationship and its threat to the traditionally more important relationship between parents and sons. Fathers are no longer sure of how much authority they have and do not care to risk asserting it with these strangers until they can do so through their sons. Mothers are ambivalent about the membership of their sons' wives in their families even when the sons are present and can be used to control them. Moreover, girls who have worked think and act differently, and many older people are afraid they will not be able to cope with them.

Although the period between engagement and marriage is often a time of worry and not a few misgivings on the part of both sets of parents, for a young woman it can be one of the pleasantest years of her life. A boy and girl who knew each other only slightly or not at all before they became engaged may visit each other and become better acquainted. Some of the bolder country girls even go into Taipei with their fiancés to attend Sunday-afternoon movies. A twenty-eight-year-old mother of three children I talked to in 1968 told me that she had never laid eyes on her husband until the day of her wedding, but she pointed with apparent pride to her young sister-in-law, whom she considered "very modern." The sister-in-law and her husband had actually had dates alone—after they were engaged, of course. There still are a good many young women who do not feel comfortable alone with a young man, even if it is the young man they are properly licensed to spend the rest of their lives with. Apparently there are even more young men who find it both an embarrassment and a strain to spend an evening "amusing" themselves with respectable fiancées.

Perhaps the most humane innovation in the often painful process of engagement and marriage is the invitation of future daughters-in-law to visit their fiancés' homes for a few days at a time during the period between engagement and marriage. Often these invitations, which are initiated by the prospective mother-in-law, are couched in terms of the mother needing some help for a seasonal activity or feast day, but their real purpose is to allow the young woman to meet some of her future relatives, perhaps learn a few of the household routines, and generally alleviate the most common terror of mankind, the fear of the unknown. In 1959 these visits were common enough not to cause raised eyebrows, but not common enough to become required. In at least two cases in Peihotien the visits resulted in a pregnant bride, but aside from causing a little amusement among the neighbors, the brides' girth was an additional source of happiness for the husbands' families. However much of a strain these visits may be at the time, they give the young bride at least some impression of the place in which she must spend the rest of her life and the people with whom she will be spending it. This is a tremendous improvement over the ordeal her mother faced on her wedding day. Unfortunately, a good many girls still "enter the sedan chair" to step out into a family of strangers.

As a mother goes about helping her daughter prepare the items of her dowry, memories of her own marriage must often come to mind. If mother and daughter have not been particularly good friends in the past, the older woman's sympathy encourages the younger to turn to her more and more during their last year together. If the mother is not at the same time worrying about financing a son's marriage, she will be cutting all possible corners to add extras to her daughter's dowry, as likely as not without the knowledge of the father. The father, for his part, though he may be going through agonies of his own at the loss of a favored daughter, must begrudge every penny spent on the dowry, a wealth that will be lost to his family forever. Insofar as he is a respectable man, a Taiwanese must never forget that he is only manager of the family's property during his lifetime. The property is not his to squander; it belongs to his ancestors and to his descendants. Even if he personally thinks his daughters are worth ten times as much as his sons, he cannot take what does not belong to him and give it to the wives of "outsiders." The mother has no such compunctions; she has always thought of herself as an "outsider" in her husband's family and considers her uterine family, the family composed of her children, the people to whom she is obliged. As long as she does not endanger her sons, she has few qualms about using the wealth of her husband's ancestors to ease her daughter's entry into adult life.

In a girl's early years the typically strained relationship between her mother and grandmother was something that she accepted without a second thought, and perhaps exploited from time to time. But when she begins to worry about her own fate at the hands of the mother-in-law to whom she is shortly to be delivered, her mother's difficulties take on a new significance. They are no longer the usual problems between her grandmother and her mother, but problems between a wife and a mother-in-law. Her mother's complaints and descriptions of past injustices suddenly receive a more sympathetic hearing and, if grandmother is still alive, may be nicely balanced by grandmother's tales of her own mother-in-law. All of which may be useful in teaching the girl some tried and true techniques for mother-in-law handling, but also probably serves to frighten her even more thoroughly.

Considering that little girls are introduced to chores and household routines much earlier than their brothers, it is surprising how ill-equipped many brides are with the basic skills necessary to run a house. In urban and wealthy families this ignorance might be explained by the presence of servants. In the country there are few servants, but several other explanations are possible. Some families have adopted daughters who do the work; other families have married sons whose wives do all the cooking and housework. And the chores assigned to little girls do not give them a particularly broad experience. Usually they mind younger children and fetch and carry. Village mothers feel far too harried to teach a child to cook a dish from beginning to end. Some children can learn by watching and do the task well enough on the first try to be allowed to repeat it. Others cannot, or do not have the interest (or courage) to try. Few are rewarded for trying—they are, in fact, likely to be punished. The following observation of a mother's irritable handling of a child trying to learn is typical. Kim-kui was cleaning a fish by the well in the yard. When she laid the knife down, her daughter picked it up and started to clean the fish head, carefully mimicking her mother's hand movements. The mother said to her, sarcastically, "You *are* busy, aren't you," and pulled the knife away from the little girl. The child continued to wash the head of the fish and some fish eggs. Later, after the mother had cut the fish into pieces and was washing each piece, the child also picked up a piece and began washing it. The mother shouted at her, "Don't use that to wash the rocks," implying unfairly that the child was dragging the fish around on the rocks. The girl put the fish down and ran into the house, returning with a brush. She scrubbed the cutting board. The mother again spoke harshly to her: "Why do you have to be getting into everything?" The child ignored her and continued to scrub on the board.

Most mothers admit that the year between engagement and marriage would be the proper time for an intensive course in the domestic arts, but I know of no mother who gave one. In this context, the proverb "It is too late to pierce the bride's ears after she is in the sedan chair" is often quoted. Basically, mothers seem to feel that their daughters should have as much freedom as possible during this, their last year at home. "Besides," they say, "their mothers-in-law will teach them." True enough, but their mothers-in-law will also be irritated at having to do so. Everyone assumes that everyone else teaches her daughter the domestic arts before marriage, and thus all have grounds for being righteously indignant with an incompetent daughter-in-law.

As the date for the wedding draws closer, mother and daughter become busier and tenser. The bride's dress is chosen, and the groom's family (who rents it) is notified of its whereabouts. Against all the rules of traditional Taiwanese color symbolism, brides now nearly all substitute white Western-style wedding dresses for the old-fashioned red gowns. As might be expected, the rented dresses often look sleazy and not quite clean. Various other items of clothing must be made, both for the bride's trousseau and for other members of the family. The bundles and boxes begin to accumulate in the hallways and bedrooms of the bride's house as gifts and dowry purchases arrive. The bride's mother's brother gives her a feast, and if she is a factory girl, her girl friends organize outings in her honor. The go-between is in and out of the house, explaining this detail, checking out that detail, and keeping both parties informed.

A day that is "good" for both families and also "good" for transporting dowries is found in the almanac,* usually from one to three days prior to the wedding day. The final hours before the departure of the dowry are frantic ones in the bride's home. Each item in the dowry must be pinned separately to bright red trays in a way that will enhance the size of the dowry and display it to advantage, although minimal care is taken to prevent damage.† When at last the dowry is completely loaded and led off on its circuitous route by the go-between, a curious emptiness is felt in the house. A proverb says, "A daughter's marriage is like a thief getting into the house." But besides the emptying of boxes and goods, there is the feeling that the girl's departure has begun, that nothing now can delay it further.

American weddings retain a few funny little rituals, such

---

* Almanacs are published each year containing, among other things, such vital information as "good days" for marrying, moving, sending dowries, and so forth. Every household has at least one, and refers to it often.

† I noted that in one case the mirror of a dresser was carefully covered with soft red corduroy (to which were pinned rosettes made from red NT $5 bills) and assumed that this was to protect it. It was not. A mirror must be covered lest someone who is pregnant or in mourning glance into it and meet serious misfortune.

as the "something old, something new; something borrowed, something blue" stricture that most brides continue to adhere to largely for the fun of it. It is hard to know which if any of the far more numerous customs in a Taiwanese wedding are done "just for fun." While I was living in Sanhsia, my interpreter and I were invited to serve as wedding attendants to a friend's young relative. It was a moving as well as an informative experience. The things I expected to be routine, such as the bowl of noodles and a chicken leg (symbolizing a wish for long life and wealth) that the mother served to the bride as she was being dressed, brought tears to both of their eyes. By the same token, the elaborate precautions I had been told of for keeping the bride from touching the earth or being seen by Heaven on her wedding day, turned out to be mainly show. When I arrived at the bride's house she had not yet returned from the hairdresser and when she did arrive, she came on her own two feet. Nonetheless, later in the ceremony, when it was necessary to transport her from a sedan chair to a taxicab, one brother carried her while another held an umbrella over her.

The arrival of the groom and his party to claim the bride quickens the pace of activity. The party is served a sweet riceball soup that the bride's attendants have been drinking unenthusiastically. The groom's soupbowl has a soft-boiled egg in it, and he is expected to break the yolk, symbolically breaking his bride's ties with her family. Although I have never seen it happen, I was told that occasionally a strong-willed mother will so overcook the egg that the groom must struggle to break the yolk and claim his bride. The go-between then calls the couple to the family altar to bow first to the gods and then to the girl's father's ancestors. At this point the sedan chair (still used by many families in Sanhsia, since taxis cannot get up mountain paths) is carried into the living room, and parents and daughter begin to exchange the ritual formulas of farewell, wishing each other long life, wealth, happiness, and for the bride, many sons. By this time mother and daughter are weeping uncontrollably. The father or his representative hands the sedan chair bearers an *ang pau*, and the bearers lower the handles of the chair so the bride may enter. The chair is closed, and the bearers carry it out of the house. The house doors are quickly slammed behind the bride's chair to prevent the wealth of the family from following the bride. Her brother spits or throws water on the departing chair to indicate that just as spilt water cannot be returned to the container, so the bride cannot return to her natal home — a thoroughly demoralizing statement, no matter how ritualized.

The wedding caravan is led by the go-between, dressed in her best and very much in charge of the situation. She is followed by a bearer carrying meat on a stock to feed to any hungry tiger that may threaten to devour the defenseless bride. A brother accompanies the bride part of the way to her new home, but her parents do not even go out the door to see her off. She is also accompanied by several female attendants, who carry the part of the groom's gifts that must be returned and a packet containing a pig's heart, a piece of meat with skin and bone clinging to it, and some sugar. From these ingredients the bride (actually, her attendants) must prepare a dish for her husband's family to eat shortly after her arrival so that they may all be "of one heart." Although a few wedding customs are carried out perfunctorily, Taiwanese weddings have not degenerated into simply a feast, as have the weddings of mainlanders displaced on Taiwan. Taiwanese are very relaxed about setting and keeping times for appointments, but the exact time of entry into the groom's house is calculated by a fortuneteller, and even the taxi drivers get nervous if they are cutting it too close. If the party arrives early, everyone sits in the street until the proper moment arrives. We saw one poor bride sitting for half an hour in a pedicab in front of her future home, taunted by children and nearly fainting from the heat in a closed vehicle on a summer afternoon. Before anyone steps from the vehicles a few handfuls of unhusked rice are thrown on them to counteract any evil that might come from someone inadvertently breaking a taboo. A small boy carrying a tray with two oranges then approaches the sedan chair and offers the bride an orange. She puts an *ang pau* on the tray and may then alight. In the old days the groom would first kick the side of the sedan chair to frighten the bride and make her obedient. The bride carried a fan, which she was to flourish in his face as a response. We were told that this custom has been dropped completely now because the cabdrivers get very upset about grooms kicking the sides of their cars. As the couple and their party enter the house they are reminded not to step on the threshold, the symbolic counterpart of the head of the house. The reminder is often visual as well, with red paper being pasted over it to serve as a protection in case someone forgets.

The bride is guided through the seemingly empty house by an old woman whose husband is still alive and who has many living and prosperous sons. The route has been cleared of the relatives, particularly the mother-in-law, so as not to frighten the bride. Any female member of the family who was born in the Year of the Tiger must be absent for the entire day because tigers are known to eat children and would threaten the fertility of the pair. Any pregnant member of the family is also expected to keep out of sight, since the meeting of two persons in an auspicious state, a double happiness, is dangerous to both. (The danger in a double happiness applies also to two brides; if two wedding processions should meet, the brides must exchange flowers for their own protection.) Once inside the room prepared for the newlyweds, the bride is in a temporary refuge; for that day at least the mother-in-law is not supposed to enter. However, after a short rest and while still in her wedding finery, the bride is summoned by her parents-in-law to the hall containing the family altar, where she and her husband solemnly bow to the ancestors. The bride is then ushered back to her room and there changes out of the white wedding dress into another elaborate dress, often an evening gown no matter what the hour of the day and usually red.

The bride is more or less confined to her room for the rest of the day. She usually has brought bags of candy and snacks for her attendants to munch on, but she is expected to eat nothing. Many young women are so frightened that they cannot eat, the obvious origin of the fast, but in at least one wedding I observed, the bride admitted that she was ravenously hungry, and when no one in her husband's family was looking she ate handfuls of the snacks provided for her attendants. The bride's attendants are given lunch, and in their absence she and the groom have a special meal, which is served to them by the go-between in a quite literal sense. The go-between serves them with her chopsticks all the while reciting auspicious phrases, dealing almost entirely with fertility, but also with longevity and happiness. The fertility theme dominates the bride's attendants' luncheon, where the older guests drink to occasionally lascivious toasts that bewilder the younger girls. The bridegroom is expected to appear and toast each of the guests, but the bride is spared this ordeal until the evening banquet, when all the family's relatives and guests gather to view her and rejoice in the prospect of a new generation. Sometimes these banquets in the homes of farmers feed over a hundred people, leaving the family on the edge of poverty.

At the end of the feast the bride and groom are led to each senior relative to bow and accept an *ang pau*, the contents of which are considered the bride's property. The couple then retire to their room, where they may be tormented for a while by young relatives and friends who are expected to make witty jokes at their expense. If the bride has done well through the day, she will have said little, smiled not at all, wept only when alone, and never, never showed any irritation. This last teasing may be the most difficult because it is often the most anxiety-provoking. Since her engagement the bride has been inundated with wishes for fertility and proverbs about descendants. At this point, when the joking is aimed at the as yet mysterious act of creating life, and at the end of an exhausting day of anxiety and uncertainty, the reminder that she must now undergo an ordeal of which she has only heard ill may be the final straw. For the young bride who in all her life has probably not spent more than a few hours without the support and companionship of her mother, sisters, or girl friends, it must be a very lonely moment.

Sex is a topic that we found the most difficult of all to interview about. Adult women were quite willing to discuss the low morals of their neighbors, and old crones even indulged in sexual joking, but reference to their own sex life brought embarrassment and a change of topic. This reticence is apparently not reserved for foreign anthropologists. Every woman our assistants could pry information out of insisted, and often with bitterness, that their mothers had told them nothing to prepare them for their first sexual experience. One woman told us that if she had known, she would never have submitted to marriage. That in itself may be the reason mothers do not tell their daughters what is expected of them in their husband's bed. More likely it is the same attitude that keeps mothers from teaching their about-to-be-married daughters some of the domestic skills that would keep them out of trouble with their mothers-in-law. They wish to spare them any knowledge of what is at least by custom an unpleasant act. It is hard to believe that farm girls who have observed copulating pigs have not wondered about the noises they hear on the sleeping platforms they share with their parents. But regardless of the conclusions they may have reached, they have learned not to ask questions. Parents make little attempt to answer children's questions on most topics and even punish them for asking too persistently. Whatever the reason, even country girls seem to find their wedding nights a miserable ordeal. One young woman we knew developed an hysterical paralysis in her legs during the weeks immediately after her marriage. Very few girls have trouble behaving with the passivity that is expected of them in their relations with their husbands.

There is a story often told when one interviews about weddings that in the old days, when families only had candles for light, a bride might not recognize her husband for some weeks after their marriage. He came to her only after dark, and in the day he avoided her as much as the other men in the house did. She of course left her room only to help with chores and always with downcast eyes. This story probably never had much truth to it, but as a symbol of the strangeness and isolation that are so much a part of a new bride's life, it has meaning. Very little is expected of her for the first few days after her entry into the family—mainly she is expected to stay in her room and be displayed to visiting relatives and curious neighbors. Three days after the wedding her younger brother comes to escort her home on a formal visit to her parents. She comes as a guest. Although she and her mother and sisters have an opportunity to spend a few hours crying and consoling one another, she is still treated as a guest with emphasis on her new status as a married woman from another family. Her home visit may be for a day or for several weeks, but it terminates when her husband comes to fetch her home. He is honored with a feast and the couple is presented with some gifts, the most important of which is a pair of shrubs renowned for their prolific production of blossoms. When the couple reach home, the senior generation offers the flowers and oily rice (a gift used to announce the birth of a child) to the Bed Mother, the little deity who watches over the children of the household. Until the bride produces a son for the family, not a day will go by without her being reminded in some way that her reason for existence is to do just that.

ᗷ 9 ᗗ

Waiting

A Taiwanese marriage is not conceived of in terms of a man taking a wife, but of a family calling in a daughter-in-law, and every bride is well aware that pleasing her husband is the least of her concerns, that it is her mother-in-law's face she must watch. In the first few years of marriage a woman spends far more of her time interacting with her mother-in-law than with her husband. If she has married a firstborn son, her mother-in-law may be in need of household help and may welcome the new bride's assistance no matter how poorly trained she is. If the older woman has no daughters or if they have all married out, she may welcome the girl as much for company as for help. The honeymoon period, which for Westerners is a husband-and-wife phenomenon, occurs in China between mother-in-law and daughter-in-law. We heard the following conversation between two mothers-in-law about a third woman whose son had recently married. "The other day I asked her if her daughter-in-law had returned to work. She told me, 'She came and asked me if she should go back to work. She said, "Mother, everyone is looking for a job and the factory is holding mine for me. I don't think I should give it up, do you? I can still cook breakfast, and if you could cook lunch when I get home from work, I'll cook the dinner. All right, Mother?"' Really, that woman is too much. She brags that when the girl gets home from work she changes her clothes right away and starts washing the family's clothes. She gets up early and sweeps the house out and cooks before she goes out to work. She told Siu-ing all of these things, and it made Siu-ing so mad that she went home and scolded her daughter-in-law for being so slow. Kim-ki shouldn't go around making everyone else mad at their daughter-in-law." The second woman replied, "Don't worry. She'll be scolding her in another month or two." And in fact Kim-ki and her daughter-in-law were quarreling bitterly before the year was out. Their fall came as a relief to all of the village women, both young and old, not because they wished the family ill, but because the earlier state of affairs was not normal. It raised questions best left unasked.

Many mothers are reluctant to marry their daughters to an eldest son because it means more work (assuming he has siblings) and because the eldest son is more likely to have his mother in his home for as long as she lives. However, the wife of an eldest son does have a somewhat better chance of finding a tolerant mother-in-law, or at least one with an open mind. No matter how bad a woman's relations with her own mother-in-law or how many neighborhood quarrels she has witnessed, she usually approaches her first daughter-in-law with hopes for good relations. And the girl, who has been frightened by stories about angered mothers-in-law, often begins her life in her new home with an unnatural meekness, never sitting in her mother-in-law's presence and always displaying what she knows of the other old-fashioned courtesies. Obviously, under the pressure of working together in the close quarters of a Taiwanese kitchen, neither woman can maintain forever a facade that does not come easily to her. The girl's casual habits with small change, the mother-in-law's insistence on cooking a vegetable the way she has always cooked it, and perhaps the increasing frequency of the girl's requests for visits home build up resentments on each side until one day they must be expressed. Unfortunately, the first outburst often does not simply ease the pressure but instead marks the end of polite relations and sets a new pattern of behavior—disapproving looks and critical comments delivered to the back of a sullen-faced young woman, or continual bickering, punctuated by sharp exchanges.

Ostensibly, one of the advantages of marrying a girl to a secondborn son is that the mother-in-law's nature is "known" (by way of her neighbors' gossip). But there can be very real disadvantages. The mother-in-law who has already had one sobering experience with a daughter-in-law is likely to expect the worst of all subsequent daughters-in-law. The "experienced" mother-in-law will begin more sternly and be decidedly less patient with the second girl than she was with the first. Moreover, the second daughter-in-law enters a household already strained by the troubles between the eldest son's wife and his mother.

The tensions in any household are bound to be quite high immediately after a second bride enters simply because of the event itself. Taiwanese weddings, as we have seen, are ruinously expensive, costing as much as a year's income. Stringent economies are made both before and after the wedding, and without a doubt these economies affect the first daughter-in-law. Human nature being what it is, she is likely to resent the young bride, whose entry cost so much. One day we were visiting in a house that had recently brought in a wife for the second son. We commented on a dresser standing in the hall, whereupon the eldest son's wife kicked it angrily and said: "It is here because there is no room for it, that's why. We must share a room now with my husband's parents so that *they* [meaning the newlyweds] can have our room. They keep the door locked all the time just as if they were trying to make the point that they have a room and we don't. She has it best. She doesn't cook, she doesn't clean vegetables, she doesn't do anything. All she does is sleep."

This is an extreme case, just as the very filial subservient young woman who silently serves every whim of her parents-in-law is the other extreme. The usual family adjustment during this period rests somewhere in between, being eased or complicated by the personality of each family member. But no matter what the quality of her later adjustment, these first few months are extremely lonely and very trying for a young woman who has never been away from home before. Even if her husband has sisters near her age, they never seem to provide the relief that might be expected in casual friendships. As often as not, the new daughter-in-law relieves the family's daughter of some of her chores; yet curiously the unmarried girl seems resentful of her intrusion into the family circle. The only real solace is provided by the children of the family. The bride's sisters-in-law may resent the money it cost to bring her into the family, but if they are typical harried mothers, they do not resent her tending their crying babies or distracting their whining children.

The men of the household are irrelevant to the life of a new bride. She is expected to obey her father-in-law and see that he is brought whatever he wants, but usually his commands are issued through his wife. The young bride is expected to leave any room he enters if she is alone. Unless in the company of some other woman of the household, the bride is even more circumspect in the presence of her husband's adult brothers. Except in bed she will not see much more of her husband. A properly behaved girl will not converse with her husband in public if it can be avoided, and if her husband spends any more time than is necessary in their bedroom, he must bear a great deal of rough teasing. Those few marriages in which the couple were well acquainted beforehand are somewhat different simply because the young woman is more comfortable in her husband's presence than in anyone else's. For most brides, husbands are little comfort. As we have seen, love marriages usually come about in such a way that the couple know each other little better than if their parents had arranged the marriage. The girl who married for love suffers not only from her mother-in-law's ill will in the early months of her married life, but from her own disillusionment as well. The young god she thought she was marrying shocked her on her wedding night, and on every day subsequent to it has proved himself quite human—in behavior she had not noticed in the romantic haze of their courtship.

At the same time that the new bride is becoming acquainted with her husband's family, she is meeting and being judged by the women's community of the village. Unless she is so fortunate as to have relatives of her own in the village, her first acquaintances among the village women are relatives or friends of her husband's mother or sisters-in-law. Gradually she gets to know a few young women of similar "outsider" status and develops her own friendships. A few familiar faces in the village go a long way toward making the loneliness and homesickness of the first few months of marriage at least bearable, but these friendships are important for other reasons as well. In the past, when a mother-in-law's authority over her daughter-in-law was more complete, village opinion was a powerful force for justice. Even today a son or a husband finds it difficult to interfere in a conflict between a woman and her daughter-in-law. But every group of women gathered around a neighborhood well to clean vegetables is a jury, and every jury has some middle-aged women on it who will make their verdict widely known. In the young woman's first few months in the village, when even her new clothes make it obvious that she is an outsider, she has no "friends at court" and can expect to come off poorly should her mother-in-law decide to air her complaints, but few families run into trouble that soon. By the end of the year, a young woman should have enough friends in the village to at least make her side of any conflict public. The women's community will nearly always favor the older woman because of her seniority in years and residence, but often the knowledge that her treatment of her daughter-in-law is under discussion is enough to put a stop to abuses commonly condemned by village gossip. Even a woman who is a long-time resident will not risk her position in the community over a minor tiff with her daughter-in-law. The women's community is too important to women of all ages for any of them to ignore its opinion. When properly mobilized by a determined woman, it can bring tremendous pressure on the male half of village society, displaying an at least apparent solidarity that the men, splintered by conflicting loyalties to descent groups, sworn brotherhoods, business and religious associations, as well as friends, cannot muster. I doubt that any bride entering a village family is ever rejected outright by the women's community, but each will be categorized as silly or sensible on the basis of her early behavior, and this label will stick for a long time.

For most families the first year after a new bride's arrival is one of peace; it is also one of waiting. The emphasis on fertility in the marriage rituals is not simply a survival from the old days. Most members of the senior generation still say quite frankly that the function of a daughter-in-law is to provide descendants. An enormous amount of money has been spent to bring in a girl capable of extending the family another generation, and any delay is certain to cause anxiety. In 1958, Taiwan's country people were well aware of the population explosion, or as they saw it, that more and more of their children were living. They were eager for birth-control information. But they were interested in limiting the number of children only after they had had three or four, at least two of whom were sons. A young man's parents were just as anxious about his new bride's ability to bear children as their great-grandparents had been. Too many children is a problem, but no descendants is a disaster.

For generations Taiwanese have been saying that ancestor worship would die out when the older generation was gone, but there is as yet no sign of that happening. Many middle-aged men admit that as young men they were determined to abandon the tradition when the responsibility for its continuation became theirs, yet when the time came this proved more difficult than they had expected. Few people believe in the literal dependence of the ancestors on the sacrifices of the living, but to discontinue the ceremonies completely leaves most Taiwanese with an uneasy feeling. It is not, after all, only some vaguely conceived godlike figures called "ancestors" to whom a farmer is burning incense each morning and evening, but a beloved grandmother who comforted him when everyone else was too busy to notice his tears. A man's ancestors include people he has known and loved as well as symbolic representations of his descent line. As the head of his family a Taiwanese farmer is responsible not only for the welfare of the living and of dead family members he remembers and mourns, but also for the welfare of members of his descent line he knows only as names in the family genealogy. Although he perhaps continues to burn incense for them simply as a gesture of personal respect and is unconcerned about the welfare of his own soul after death, his desire for sons remains strong. They have for too long been a sign of wealth and prestige, a symbol of stability and respectability. A young man wants to see his first child born because in many ways it is only then that he becomes fully adult. He may always remain a child to his parents, but to the community and to his wife he becomes the father of Thian-su. A young woman wants a baby because she has been told that her reason for existence is to produce one, because the family pressure on her to do so is uncomfortably urgent, and because she is desperately lonely. Grandfathers want to see the new generation before they die because they want to see their family continue and prosper; grandmothers want the more personal pleasure of babies they can love and even spoil with impunity.

In the country we were often told that a woman who failed to produce children would be returned to her family, but no one could point out such a woman or introduce us to a family that had sent a barren bride home. In farm families the expense and trouble of replacing a bride is too great. Nonetheless, the threat remains—along with the perhaps worse fate of remaining in her husband's family childless. Until a young woman becomes the mother of one of the family's sons, she feels very insecure. As the rituals of her wedding day made clear, she retains few claims on her father's family, and unless she bears a child for her husband's family, she will have no rights there. She *wants* to become pregnant, and if she is married to the eldest son she is made to feel she *must* become pregnant. Her mother-in-law begins asking embarrassingly blunt questions about her menstrual cycle and allows her to overhear the disgusted comments she makes to her friends. The watchful eyes of village women with few other interests take note of any swelling of her breasts or expanding of her waistline and as the months go by comment questioningly on the absence of such symptoms.

A mother-in-law with no grandchildren will not be able to restrain herself for long. Some action is called for, and it usually involves a visit to the *tang ki*. A *tang ki* is a religious practitioner who serves as an intermediary for a god. The god takes possession of the *tang ki*'s body and speaks through him to the suppliants. People come to the *tang ki* to ask his god for help in finding lost items, curing sick people and animals, changing a family's economic fortune, settling quarrels with relatives or friends, and solving the problem of infertility in pigs and brides. Usually the cause of a misfortune is discovered to be a ghost or a supernatural troublemaker from popular mythology who must be placated with offerings, but the *tang ki*'s prescription is often more commonsensical than his diagnosis. We have heard more than once of a *tang ki* who advised a client to consult a medical doctor, and on one sad occasion we listened to a *tang ki* advise an old lady to go home and prepare mourning clothes. He had "saved" her aged husband once before, but the old man had now lived far beyond his allotted years.

In every *tang ki*'s session (they hold regular hours much like doctors in a medical clinic), there is always a worried looking middle-aged lady who has come to ask what to do about a daughter-in-law who is not showing signs of pregnancy. The *tang ki* usually tells the woman to bring the girl at once to have her "flower fortune" examined. The childbearing potential of every woman is represented by a supernatural flowering tree. The strength of the blossoms on the tree (white ones for sons and red ones for daughters), whether they will shrivel in the bud or survive to bloom, depends on many things. Several kinds of animal spirits—tigers, monkeys, birds—may eat the buds; the soil the tree grows in may be of poor quality or the water insufficient; or the soul of a pregnant woman who entered the nuptial chamber may cause the buds to fall before they can bloom. Happily, most of these misfortunes can be successfully treated by the *tang ki* once the girl is present. The next step is to present the daughter-in-law.

After the girl's supernatural flowers have been ritually examined, cleaned, cultivated, or even changed, her mother-in-law will relax for a while. Few farm families would consider visiting a medical doctor until they had exhausted the traditional techniques. There is a particular kind of Kuan-im (the Buddhist Goddess of Mercy) who appears in a few temples— I know of one in Taipei and another in Tainan—and is reputed to be able to help barren women seeking her help. Asking help from other gods is considered by most women to be too dangerous. With much begging the god might decide to send the suppliant a child, but it would not really be the family's child, would probably be deformed, and certainly would not live to fulfill its obligations as a child of the family. It would be the god's child and only loaned to the beseeching family out of pity.

At some point a neighbor or a relative is going to tell the mother-in-law of a bride with a flat stomach about a healthy, attractive, baby girl someone wants to adopt out. A few decades ago the mother-in-law might have gone to inspect the child, discussed the price asked with her husband, and then brought the baby home without so much as a nod to the young woman's desires in the matter. In modern Taiwan any woman who has tolerable relations with her daughter-in-law will consult her at each step. Adopting a female child is neither difficult nor expensive in Taiwan, and although adoption is not as frequent as it once was, it is still a common practice. A little girl is brought into a childless family not as a substitute for children born to the family but "to lead in a son." There does seem to be some evidence, albeit inconclusive, that women who have been labeled barren are more likely to conceive after they adopt children.* Apparently, the simple reduction of tensions produces a biochemical change that increases the likelihood of conception. The Chinese have found the practice to be particularly efficacious, perhaps because they often make this kind of adoption so early that there has been no real test of the woman's (or her husband's) fertility. The adoption of a baby girl does not relieve the young bride's anxieties about her ability to provide the family with the one

---

* See William C. Weir and David R. Weir, "Adoption and Subsequent Conceptions," *Fertility and Sterility*, 17, 2 (1966), for a discussion of the evidence and further references.

thing it wants from her, sons, but the introduction of a child into a family without children often changes the climate of the group. The girl and her husband have a legitimate topic for relaxed conversation. The parents-in-law can enjoy the presence of a grandchild and feel that they are doing all *they* can to fulfill their obligations to their ancestors. And the "mother" has a child to hold when the other women gather to chat with their babies on their backs, a child to fondle and console when she herself feels utterly alone and friendless.

Most of the young women who married into Peihotien rewarded the watching villagers within a very few months with a certain puffiness around the eyes, a tightness in the bodice, and finally, a skirt that no longer fastened. Pointedly questioning glances directed to the mother-in-law produce a satisfied nod of agreement. The brides themselves are likely to be so overcome with embarrassment by a direct question that they will deny the obvious or, to avoid the topic, flee. How much of this is act and how much of it real is hard to say. Whichever, it is a happy embarrassment, and the entire family, particularly if awaiting the first representative of a new generation, is likely to take on a considerably more friendly countenance toward one another and toward the outside world. The mother-in-law will have endless bits of advice to give on backaches, swelling feet, and the alteration of clothes. If the husband's grandmother is still alive and mentally active, she will provide innumerable prescriptions and restrictions that were practiced in *her* day and *should* be continued. No matter how ridiculous these nostrums may seem, the mother-to-be finds them and everything pertaining to pregnancy very interesting. A first pregnancy mends many breaches in the relations between a young wife and her mother-in-law, the girl out of need and the older woman out of delight at the prospect of a grandson.

There are many restrictions placed on a pregnant woman,

but few of them are for the protection of the mother. Her diet is not supplemented to assist her body in its task of building another. Unless she has been doing unusually strenuous work, she is not encouraged to be less active. In fact, nearly all of the restrictions placed on a pregnant woman are designed to protect the fetus, not the mother. The little god Thai-sin becomes a major character in the household's daily planning. An old lady told me that a truly virtuous woman consults the almanac before she does anything, particularly when she is pregnant. Thai-sin is a vindictive little god who moves about a great deal. The almanac tells which room of the house or part of the yard he is in on any given day. If Thai-sin is in the bedroom and out of ignorance or arrogance a pregnant woman should sew in that room, she might poke the little god in the eye. In retribution her child will be born blind. If a knife or other sharp instrument is used in the room Thai-sin is visiting, the child may be born with a cleft palate. In Sanhsia I was shown a child with a sadly deformed hand, the result of her mother's crocheting fish nets (a cottage industry) in Thai-sin's presence. A woman in her forties and her new daughter-in-law interviewed me one day about the frequency of cleft lips in the United States. I assumed they wanted to know if the deformity was operable. No, indeed. They were interested in whether Thai-sin was also in the United States, and this was the most obvious evidence. Another woman gave as evidence of Thai-sin's power the fact that even the Japanese feared him. The Japanese colonial administration held regular house inspections to ensure a minimum standard of cleanliness, but made exceptions for the room of a pregnant woman out of consideration for Thai-sin.

Thai-sin is not the only supernatural threat to a pregnant woman. Taoist ceremonies of any sort are dangerous. Before a Taoist priest begins to perform in a home, the family sends someone to warn pregnant women in the neighborhood to close their doors. The ritualized act of driving nails into a coffin is also considered very dangerous. In fact, if a death occurs in the family a pregnant woman must wear a particular kind of mourning cloth around her abdomen to protect the unborn child. Some midwives recommend that in a first pregnancy a young woman be encouraged to eat food from wedding and funeral feasts and from a woman "within the month." If she does this, she will be free from restrictions in later pregnancies and will not have to worry about endangering the fetus by unwittingly eating food contaminated by ritual. Frankly, I doubt that many women would encourage or even allow a daughter-in-law to risk their unborn grandson with such measures. Many will not even allow her to take routine medicines (such as aspirin) for fear of harming the fetus. Pregnant women are warned not to kill animals of any kind. "The animal may be coming to be reborn again, so that if you kill it you will kill your baby. Sometimes a mother sees the animal or person who is coming to be reborn, and other people standing right next to her do not. Even if you catch a rat in your house, you must let it go."

For her own family, a pregnant woman is a source of joy and, if it is her first child, of relief, but for other members of the community she can be a danger. She must not share her bed with another pregnant woman, or their children may be "exchanged." As we noted in another context, when a bride first enters her new home, pregnant women must leave the house. They should in fact not even enter the room prepared for a new bride. The presence of a pregnant woman or a member of her family can also cause serious injury at a firewalk to the men who carry the gods across the hot beds of coals. But her most consistent threat is to children. Any other children she has are expected to be comparatively *kui khi* during her pregnancy. And friends and neighbors are less than happy if she handles their children too much. If a pregnant woman hugs or holds someone else's child she may only make him irritable or mopey for a few days, but if her unborn child is particularly "fierce," a serious illness may result. If she accidentally frightens a child, she should give his parents a length of ribbon from her hair to tie around the child's wrists as an amulet. Sometimes all of a woman's own children will wear these little bracelets as protective devices.

During the last month of pregnancy, a woman must not venture far from home, for as we noted in Chapter 5, the only proper place for a child to be born is in the home of its father. When labor starts, the girl's mother is notified, if the family lives fairly close, and a midwife is summoned. In view of the crowding that is considered normal and even desirable in Chinese living, it is amazing how many young women have never witnessed a childbirth. The children of the family may be sent off to stay with neighbors, but in village life children wander in and out of houses as freely as chickens, and busy adults do not seem to notice their presence. Still, most of the young women we talked to claimed to be totally ignorant of the mechanics of childbirth when they bore their first child. One unmarried girl we heard of had assisted a friend, a partner in a love marriage who was giving birth without the help of either a mother or a mother-in-law, and was so shaken by the experience that she vowed never to marry.

Whether or not the girls have witnessed a childbirth, during the months of their pregnancy they have picked up enough information to know what is expected of them. Although they are allowed some expression during the final period of labor, hysteria, screams, or persistent crying is severely censured. A young woman who cries out is scolded both by her mother-in-law and by the midwife with such comments as, "If you don't want babies, why do you sleep with your husband?"—as if the girl had a choice in the matter. If the girl really loses control, her mother will be sent for no matter how inconvenient. She is summoned not to comfort her daughter, but to shame her and in effect to be called to account herself. Although such measures are not resorted to often, there were two women in Peihotien who had been humiliated in this way during their first labor. Their cases were frequently discussed, sometimes, I suspected, for the edification of village brides. It is by means of shame that the women's community disciplines its members. When I asked the wife of a petty official in Sanhsia if women were expected to be stoical in childbirth, she answered, "Oh, no, not anymore. Just those women who worry about what others say."

Even if the first child born to the young wife is only a girl, the family will relax. She may have disappointed them by not producing a son the first time around, but a normal, healthy baby girl at least proves her capacity to bear the family's descendants. Friends and relatives console her with the thought that it really *is* better to have a girl first so she can help take care of the children who follow, but for the young mother the baby girl is a consolation in her own right. The new mother can spend hours investigating the infant's toes and ears, and more hours comparing her surreptitiously or openly with a sister-in-law's baby or a neighbor's. She has a baby at her breast when the women congregate for a visit on a sleepy afternoon, and she has something to contribute when they begin comparing the feeding or sleeping habits of their infants.

If the young wife has borne a male child, she is now firmly established in a new status: she is the mother of one of the family's descendants. There is now very little possibility of the family's repudiating her. The Chinese stress on filiality encourages a wealth of folklore about filial sons, including stories of young men going off in search of mothers lost in their childhood. Parents-in-law would require grave cause to risk the divided loyalties of a descendant. Furthermore, public opinion would deal harshly with a family that cast out the mother of one of its descendants unless her crime was truly heinous.

The birth of a child of either sex creates a new relationship between the girl and her husband. If the marriage was a love marriage, the emotional ties have undoubtedly frayed if not entirely worn through by the end of the first year. There is little to support such ephemeral bonds in the setting of an extended country family. The presence of a child and the status of parenthood give the couple a recognized and socially acceptable relationship to fill this void and to soothe the disappointments. For the young couple who do not bear the responsibility of a love marriage, the status of parenthood may solve a good many embarrassments, not the least of which is how to address each other, and may even give them a proper framework within which to consider the pleasant emotions they have come to feel in each other's presence. Even if their attitude toward each other is somewhat less pleasant, the child is for its mother a consolation and someone to love, and for its father, both proof to the outside world of his filiality and the end of his own childhood. The young man's parents may still on occasion treat him as a child, but to the village he is a man, the father of a new generation. And no matter how distasteful he may find the wife chosen for him by his parents, he is grateful to the mother of his son.

Taking Charge

No matter how many younger brothers and sisters a young woman may have tended in childhood, her experience with newborn babies is limited. None of the babies she saw as a child looked so fragile or seemed so precious as her own. In the first weeks after her child's birth, she turns repeatedly and gratefully to her mother-in-law for advice and assistance. Often the older woman sleeps with her during the first few weeks in order to help her during the night and to make sure that the young father does not resume sexual relations with his wife too soon after childbirth. For both women this is a peaceful and happy time. The younger woman needs the advice and help, and the older woman is delighted to be intimately involved in her grandchild's care. In many families this period of shared concern sets a tone for the future relations between the two women that prevents them from ever becoming serious enemies. If they have been politely fulfilling the roles of daughter-in-law and mother-in-law, the tie of the child gives them, as it does husband and wife, a topic of conversation and an appreciation of each other's qualities.

Unfortunately, the peculiarities of the Chinese family and the limitations of human personalities usually operate against the continuation of these pleasant relations. The younger woman comes into conflict with the older one over some matter relating to the child's care or simply begins to resent her authoritative comments. When the child is a male, the strain is more intense. The young mother feels that the boy is hers, and that she must decide what is best for him. The older woman considers the child her son's son and a member of her uterine family who will burn incense for her after her death. He is far too important to be trusted to the inexperienced hands of a young mother. If the two women were left to themselves to solve their difficulties, they might be able to do so without any lasting scars, each soothed by the other's obvious appreciation of the child's qualities. But that is not the way of it. Instead, each woman looks around her for support—Taiwanese women learn young that they cannot win battles without a man as a screen. The younger woman appeals to the only person who has any reason to feel obliged to her—her husband. The older woman also seeks support from a person directly involved, a member of her own family whose loyalty she has spent much of her adult life cultivating—her son. The fact that both women appeal to the same person, a person whose support both regard as crucial, may escalate a disagreement over a minor matter of child care into the opening scene of the inevitable struggle between them for the exclusive loyalty of the young man. If the son sides with his wife, even the most level-headed mother will be hurt. A less confident woman will be more than hurt—she may see her whole future made bleak by a son who has turned away from her, possibly even the disintegration of her family. Her son is plainly being manipulated by her daughter-in-law to set up a separate household, and after all her years of devotion, she will be left alone, or at least without her son to lean on. We came in on the end of just such a quarrel in a village family. The mother-in-law threatened to kill herself and shouted bitterly, "Then the two of you will be alone and won't have a mother in your way." This is not an empty threat by women in this age group, and it clearly seemed a dangerous possibility to the woman's son. He was very upset and led his mother to a chair saying, "You are my mother. How can I let such a thing happen? If she is not nice to you, we will send her home. How could I let you kill yourself?" He turned to his wife and shouted at her, "Go home. Go home. Don't you hear me? Go tell your mother what a bad daughter-in-law you are."

For the first year or two, most sons regard their mothers as more experienced and therefore more reliable in the field of child training than their young wives. If they can convey this to their wives without offending them, they may be instrumental in preserving current family harmony and in setting the tone for the future. Usually, however, a young man is required to display this diplomacy in the midst of a highly emotional scene, and more often than not, as in the case of the young man quoted above, he curses his wife in a conventional show of filiality. A few experiences of this kind are enough to convince his wife, as her mother and her mother-in-law before her were convinced, that a woman cannot depend on her husband for support in times of trouble. To be sure, she will use every technique available to manipulate him, but when she looks to her future, she too will look to it in terms of her son, not her husband.

Both consciously and unconsciously, a woman weaves ties with her sons that are personal and exclusive. These links are not based on explicit reminders of obligations or filiality, but on emotions that call forth memories of warmth and comfort, flashes of gratitude, and pure satisfactions. To fail one's father produces shame before the outside world, but to fail one's mother has a psychological effect that is far, far more painful. To achieve this result, a mother must compromise her husband's relationship with his sons. In Chapter 5 I discussed the abrupt changes that take place in a child's life when he reaches the age of six and is considered capable of "understanding" parental training. Even the most affectionate father feels required, for the welfare of his son, to withdraw from him and become a distant awesome figure in his life. It is only from this distance that he can teach his son the virtues of obedience and respect for his elders and ancestors. A naughty child is grabbed by his mother and given a smart slap or even a painful beating. A child who has been found guilty of serious wrongdoing is punished by his father, not on the spur of the moment, but by appointment and with cool, even strokes of a bamboo rod. A father's beatings, though much less frequent and much less painful, are recalled with much more fear. A mother uses father as a threat to a recalcitrant child, and in so doing places herself constantly in the position of arbiter between the child and his father. Threats of punishment that she makes in the father's name and later retracts are remembered by the child with gratitude and with a recognition of their shared fear of the father. A woman who has suffered badly at the hands of her husband will sabotage his relations with their sons—because she has nowhere else to turn and for revenge. We were told over and over again in Peihotien that children always "knew" if their fathers wasted the family money on girl friends and other distractions. Mothers said the children had eyes and could see, but we noticed that what the children failed to see, the mothers were quick to point out. A woman who had been abandoned by her husband lived briefly in two rooms in the back of the house in which we lived in Peihotien. The neighbors felt sorry for her but even sorrier for her ten-year-old son. Whenever he got into any mischief, his emotional mother would call up all the sins of his father and contrast them with her own selflessness. Although the following quotation is lacking in ingenuity, it is an example of the style of many country women. The boy, who had spent part of the money set aside for school fees on candy, was being lectured.

You know that you are my only son, and that your father didn't take care of you. He ran away with a younger woman and left us all alone. You should know this. If you won't listen to me now, what will you be like when you are bigger? It must be that you want to make me mad so that I will die sooner, is that it? Why should I want to live so long when my life is so bitter? It is only because of you. If it weren't for you, I could just leave this world now. You won't listen to me, so perhaps I had best just go die. Then there will be no one to control you, and you will be happy. [The child began to cry and beg, "Don't, Mother. Don't." But the mother was relentless.] You know that your father ran off with that woman, and you ought to realize that your mother is the only one you have to lean on. Don't think that your father came to see you when he came that day. He just came to see if we had any money for him to spend. If I were to die, you would only have two roads open to you. Either you would have to make your own living, or you would have to go live with your father. But such a small child couldn't make his own living, and if you went to your father you would be killed by that woman. Isn't your not listening to me the same as your wanting me to die? You are my only son, and, since my husband is not a person who will help me, you are the one on whom I have to put all of my hopes. If you will not listen to me now, what hope is there for when you grow up? It would be better for me to die now.

A woman who respects her husband and is confident that he will not abandon her for a younger woman or waste the family's money and the children's future by excessive gambling does not feel as great a need to bind her sons to her, and therefore is not as likely to be as destructive to their relations with their father. She will use him as the ultimate punisher, but she will also increase his stature by showing her deference to him, referring problems to his authority, and by interpreting his behavior in such a way as to make it more acceptable, if not wholly understandable, to his sons. She will nonetheless also make it clear to them that she is on their side of the fence.

Above: a country town. Below: a village house

Above: washing clothes and exchanging news. Below: drying rice

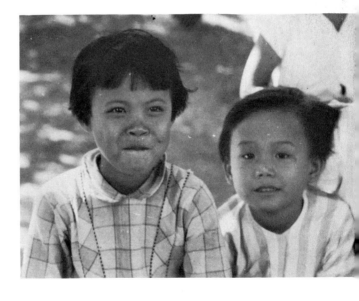

Little girls

Older girls. Above: factory girls. Below left: a filial daughter
Below right: an adopted daughter with her foster sister's children

Above: a village wedding, 1959. Below: a town wedding, 1969

Mothers and grandmothers

Above: laying out a feast for the "ghosts"
Below: burning incense at a local temple

Above: great-grandmothers
Below: mourners wailing on the coffin of an old woman

Their father may be a valued "friend of the family," but she and her children *are* the family.

To village women who have experienced empty stomachs and sewed patches on patches, disasters of one sort or another seem likely, and their resources for coping with them are very limited. They depend primarily on their sons, for in times of crisis it is well known that sons are more dependable than husbands. Any threat to a woman's relations with her son strikes deep. Suicide statistics collected during the first two decades of this century dramatically reflect the crisis periods in a woman's life. Young women in their early and middle twenties, despairing at the cruelties of their mothers-in-law and desirous of revenge (the ghost of a suicide is believed to be particularly powerful and absolutely determined to bring tragedy to the people responsible), drink poison or throw themselves off bridges or under trains, producing the highest rate of suicide for any age group. The rate then drops sharply and steadily until the fortieth year, when it rises again for women between forty and fifty, reflecting the crises created by marriages that intrude strange women into the beds and affections of sons. In the first two decades of the century, the hazardous forties were followed by a gradual decline in the suicide rate as women entered old age and settled down as respected grandmothers; but by 1930, the fifties were showing themselves to be nearly as hazardous as the forties. This rise probably reflects both the later age of marriage and the increasing difficulty the senior generations were having in controlling their offspring.

Mother-in-law–daughter-in-law conflicts do not ordinarily result in a suicide statistic. Although the dramatic quarrels ending with suicides or family divisions attract the most attention, the usual result, particularly in families with only one son, is for the two women to settle down to a pattern of occasional bickering, with the older woman gradually, sometimes begrudgingly, turning over control of the household to her young rival. As often as not the older woman enjoys her grandchildren and the ease and freedom from routine tasks that her daughter-in-law's growing competency allows her. She may quite happily turn over the majority of her responsibilities before her husband is ready to pass on his position as family leader. And unless the younger woman harbors a serious grudge against her mother-in-law, once she is confident of her own position she finds her mother-in-law's presence quite helpful. A woman with several children and a willing mother-in-law is in for a far easier time than a woman who lives alone with her husband and children. She can visit her parents with relative ease, whereas a visit by a daughter who must bring along her five children becomes an ordeal that neither mother nor daughter wants repeated too frequently.

As a result of the remarkable improvement in health conditions in Taiwan, many families now see two or even three sons survive to adulthood. The Chinese ideal, the ideal of the men's culture, is to have a family of many sons and grandsons living with their wives and children in harmony under one roof and under the authority of the senior male. Unfortunately, among the farm families we knew or knew of, the extended family rarely survived the birth of children to the second son, and if it did, it was almost sure to be divided on the death of the father. Students of other parts of China who have observed this phenomenon have laid it to competitiveness between brothers for the limited wealth of their father.* But my observations of Taiwanese families suggest to me that the emotional strains within the family, including the tensions that arise from the existence of uterine families, are the heavy

* See Maurice Freedman, *Chinese Lineage and Society* (London School of Economics Monographs on Social Anthropology, No. 33, 1966).

contributors to family division. One might expect the wife of the eldest son to welcome with open arms the bride of her husband's younger brother, particularly if she has been suffering from a domineering mother-in-law, but this is seldom the case. The older girl's resentment of the younger begins to accumulate before the younger brother's engagement ceremony is completed. Usually the wife of a son has little to say (in fact, would not dare say anything) about the financial negotiations for the marriage of another son in the family, but the demands of the bride's family are openly and heatedly discussed in the family circle. A wedding is a tremendous expense for a farm family and often causes considerable hardships for the family for a year or even longer after the event. By the time the sedan chair arrives, the eldest daughter-in-law is probably convinced that her children's future has been jeopardized by the outrageous demands of the bride's parents. Her feelings are not notably soothed when she sees some of the money her husband's family put out in bride price coming back in a gorgeous dowry for the exclusive use of the new couple—even less so if her mother-in-law makes unfavorable comparisons with what *her* parents provided. Unless the elder daughter-in-law is a paragon of good nature, and the new daughter-in-law mature beyond her years, any potential there is for a coalition between them is destroyed in the first few months, the honeymoon period between a mother-in-law and her newest daughter-in-law. I mentioned earlier how women are angered by the "goodness" of someone else's new daughter-in-law when they compare them with their own; consider, then, how it must be when this amazing creature is a member of your own household, and it is your own mother-in-law who is singing her praises. Taiwanese folklore and gossip are full of tales of older sisters-in-law who work out ingenious methods of sabotaging their competitor's good relations, from dropping sand in the rice when it is the younger woman's turn to cook to misreporting innocent comments made about the household's management.

The younger girl in her inexperience does little to ease the situation. Having been completely terrified by all she has heard about mothers-in-law, she is usually pleased with herself for so easily charming her own, and assumes that the sour face of her sister-in-law simply reflects her natural temperament. By the time the mother-in-law loses patience with the bride's ineptitudes, the girl has probably prejudiced if not made impossible cooperative relations with her sister-in-law. When her own children begin to arrive, the only solution she can see to the misery of life with an overbearing mother-in-law and an unfriendly sister-in-law is a division of the family. The elder sister-in-law, resigned to the fact that as the wife of the eldest son only death will free her of her mother-in-law, may be equally eager to divide the household if she considers the younger family a drain on their joint resources. Both women carry tales, highly colored, of the other's extravagances, of favoritism by the parents, and both exaggerate the contribution their half of the family makes to the joint budget. Unlike brothers who have been raised to value the extended family, women have learned to look first to their own interests, and after they have children, to look to their children's best interests. If the division of the family is motivated by economic considerations, I do not think it is because brothers are concerned about their children's share in their father's estate, but rather because their wives are concerned about their uterine family's share in that estate. It is the existence of uterine families within the descent group that causes its fission.

For all the adages urging the opposite, the relationship between brothers in China is often distant, and if their wives embark on a campaign aimed at family division, the brothers are soon likely to accept the worst side of each other's character as dominant. Unless the parents are particularly strong willed, division is inevitable. Usually the division does not require either branch of the family to leave the family home, but means simply setting up separate stoves, reapportioning some rooms, and closing off a door or two. Arbiters, often relatives of the mother's parents, are called in to divide the property into shares, which are drawn by lot unless the family agrees on a specific arrangement. After the allocations are made, the family sits down to a final meal together. What remains of the meal is divided into equal portions and solemnly carried from the table to the new kitchens by, significantly, the daughters-in-law.* In some families this division may produce such a change in atmosphere that relations begin to improve at once, but in others so much bitterness has accumulated that the brothers may refuse to speak to each other for years after. Relations between the sisters-in-law are not likely ever to be friendly. Brothers have the memories of the charmed circle of their uterine family to heal their damaged relations, but their wives have been first strangers and then enemies. They have no former good times to hearken back to and are therefore unlikely to ever be more than civil to each other.

For a Taiwanese farm woman, the years between thirty and forty are the busiest of her life, but also the most peaceful. Some of her children are old enough to help her in the care of the others, or at least old enough to fend for themselves during most of the day. If her mother-in-law is still with her, she is gradually entrusting her with more and more responsibilities but is still capable of carrying a good share of the burden of cooking, cleaning, child care, and the feeding of domestic animals. Although farm women in the north do not as a rule work in the fields, most women help on occasion with the

* This ceremony is described by Toshio Ikeda in *Taiwan no Katei Seikatsu* (Home Life in Taiwan), pp. 141–43 (Taipei: Toto Shoseki, 1944).

planting, weeding, and harvesting of vegetables, and nearly all farm wives take responsibility for the drying of the harvested rice, the washing of vegetables for market, and the gathering of food for the family pigs. The young bride who dreamed of outings she would take and visits she would make to her mother just as soon as she had usurped her mother-in-law's power finds herself far too busy to make more than the visits to her natal home required at New Year or for weddings and funerals. Without realizing just when, she has finally come to find the life of her husband's village more absorbing, the gossip more exciting, than events in the village where she grew up. There were so many strange faces there the last time she went back. As far as outings are concerned, she is much too tired and quite unwilling to "waste money" that will be needed for her son's new school uniform.

For some women these years bring a new kind of trouble. With the death of his father a man may be left in unquestioned charge of the family affairs, including the family finances. At this point in life a weakness for gambling and wineshops may gradually surface. What his mother assumed was the normal experimentation of a young man may in middle age come to be a solace for the bleakness of life— a solace that a farm family usually cannot afford. His aged mother's reproach may serve only to make his need greater, and his wife's angry scenes may simply add a mistress to his expenses. As one woman explained: "If you have that kind of a husband, your whole life is going to be hard. You can't fight with him, because you will just make people laugh at your family. You can't die over him, because you don't have two lives. You can't just walk out, because you have the children. If you leave the family, people who know your husband will blame him, but people who don't will say you are a bad woman who abandoned her family. If you have a bad husband, you have a bad life." As far as most women are concerned, there is no solution. "If you have a bad *mia:* [fate], you have a bad husband. You can go home and tell your parents, and they may sympathize and let you stay a few days, but you still have to come back to him. They can't feed you and your children for the rest of your life. 'The rice is cooked,' so there is nothing that can be done." It almost goes without saying that women who find themselves in this predicament allow their husbands not one shred of respect from their children and make full use of the women's community to ensure that his abuses of the family estate are known to all. As with other kinds of dissension, the women collect the evidence, make the judgment, and then instruct their menfolk. Sometimes this loss of face will return a man to his duties, but if it does not, his wife takes some satisfaction in having publicized his fall.

Needless to say, just as not all mothers-in-law are viragoes, not all husbands are scoundrels. Most men in their thirties and forties are busy taking on their father's duties, providing for their growing family, and worrying about how many and which of their sons they can afford to educate. If a man has made a friend of his wife, he will seek her counsel on these decisions. Both husband and wife find their relations with his parents gradually changing in substance. They continue to treat the senior members of the family with respect and deference, yet find themselves thinking of them more and more often in the same category as their children—those who need, not those who provide. A man's relations with his aged parents presage his relations with them after death. He shows them respect and deference, and they are dependent on him for their sustenance.

When a woman is in her late forties, her youngest child in school and her eldest either working in a factory or with his father in the fields, the day comes when a neighbor begins to tell her with unusual animation about a young relative, emphasizing her health, good nature, and intelligence. The mother probably listens as casually as the woman washing clothes next to her, until finally the exasperated neighbor points out that the girl is but a year younger than her son and would be quite a catch. With a shock she realizes that a marriage is being proposed for her son. Although she may laugh away this suggestion, Pandora's Box is open. She begins to wonder who else works in his factory, or, if he works in the family fields, why he spends so much time hanging around the village store, the store run by a family with three teen-age daughters. When she begins to get answers to her unspoken questions, she may feel that something new and not entirely pleasant is happening in her family, but as a matter of fact she has been here before. The Chinese family is cyclical, and her family (for her uterine family and the household are nearly the same by now) is about to return to that phase of the cycle in which there are married couples in two generations. She has moved to the senior generation; she will soon be, of all things, a mother-in-law.

Girls Who Marry Their Brothers

To this point I have been discussing the lives of women who were raised by the families into which they were born and married into other families as young adults. To put it another way, I have been assuming what Arthur Wolf calls the major form of marriage.* This is the "typical" form of marriage and the one assumed by both Chinese and Western scholars of China. But as a matter of fact, over half of the marriages in the Taipei basin prior to 1925 did not require the transfer of a young woman to another household. Unfortunately, reliable statistical data are not available for other parts of China, but there is ample anecdotal and incidental evidence that the number of "atypical" marriages in other areas was nearly as high. The Ong family I described in Chapter 2 made use of both of the "non-major" forms of marriage to continue the family line. Ong Thuan-cong had no son and had to use his adopted daughter to bring in a son-in-law in an uxorilocal marriage; Cin-cai and his wife adopted a baby girl who they later married to their son in the *sim-pua* form of marriage

* Arthur P. Wolf, "Adopt a Daughter-in-Law, Marry a Sister: A Chinese Solution to the Problem of the Incest Taboo," *American Anthropologist*, 70, 5 (October 1968). I have relied heavily on Arthur Wolf for the statistical information in this chapter. In addition to the article cited, I have used both his "Childhood Association and Sexual Attraction: A Further Test of the Westermarck Hypothesis," *ibid.*, 72, 3 (June 1970) and some of his unpublished data.

(which Wolf refers to as the minor marriage). As long as the focus of interest is on the culture of the Chinese male, these two forms of marriage are simply alternate means of continuing a descent line, but for the other half of Chinese society, specifically for the uterine families of the women, the emotional climate of the domestic units, and the solidarity of the women's community, they have very different effects. In this chapter I will discuss the lives of girls who marry their foster brothers, and in the next the lives of women who are party to uxorilocal marriages.

Many crises in Taiwanese family life are resolved by the adoption of an infant. A woman whose baby dies may be given a child to ease her grief. Families who have no children and fear that they may be left without descendants adopt girls and later, if they can afford it, a boy. Sometimes a family is so anxious about descendants that a girl is adopted before a bride has been in the household a year. Even a woman who has borne a daughter or two may be presented with an adopted daughter to "lead in a son." Until recently the most common form of adoption was that of bringing in a *sim-pua* as a future daughter-in-law. Typically, a woman's newborn daughter would be given away (by her mother-in-law's arrangement) and another girl adopted-in to drink her milk. The adopted-in child would be raised as a kind of second-class daughter, and when she reached physical maturity, be quietly married to her foster brother.

Taiwanese folktales and proverbs lean heavily for their pathos on the ill-treatment of adopted daughters. Everyday expressions comment on an adopted daughter's life: a girl with a sullen expression has a face like a *sim-pua*; a sobbing child cries like a *sim-pua*; a young girl complains that her parents make her work like a *sim-pua*. From the many anecdotes we were told by and about our neighbors, it is clear that the life of an adopted daughter was not a pleasant one a generation or two ago. Even now these girls are not considered the equals of their foster siblings, but a government campaign to alleviate the worst abuses, along with a generally less tolerant attitude toward human suffering, has greatly improved their lot. Adopted daughters usually enter when families are under a cloud of unhappiness, such as the death of a child or anxiety over the possible sterility of a daughter-in-law, but even an adopted daughter who came as a *sim-pua* was not entirely welcome. A woman with a son two or three years old who gave birth to a girl was likely to find that her mother-in-law had arranged to have the infant adopted by another family, and that she was to have a *sim-pua* to take her daughter's place at her breast. Few women had sufficient milk to raise both children, and even if they did, few parents-in-law were willing to raise an extra girl who could give the family nothing but added expense. A daughter is useful if you have no sons, and every family needs one to help around the house; but an adopted daughter is also insurance in case a family should lose its sons, helps around the house far more than a mother could force her own daughter to do, and besides that can be married to the family's son to provide descendants. Few young mothers actively opposed this custom, in part because families all around them were adopting, and in part because they knew their opposition would be hopeless. They were themselves ambivalent. The reasons most commonly given for adopting a *sim-pua* were that they made such dutiful daughters-in-law, could be depended on to treat their mothers–mothers-in-law well in their old age, and were unlikely to try to come between a mother and her son. For a young mother who was just beginning her uterine family but who had already learned that it was her small son on whom she would be dependent, these were powerful arguments. Her own daughter could only be hers for a few years, and then she would belong to another family anyway.

Young women who were angered by the loss of their babies did not dare express the depth of their frustration to their mothers-in-law or even to their husbands. Unfortunately, they often found an outlet for their hostility in the child who was given to them as a *sim-pua*. A woman in her fifties told us:

Children of that time [her mother's age] often died because their foster mothers hated them and beat them. It was very hard to be a *sim-pua* then. Both of Man-ku's older brothers' wives were adopted daughters, but their foster mother didn't like one for some reason. Even when she was tiny she was always getting beaten. That woman would take the little girl and put her in a chicken basket and then set a bundle of rice stalks on fire and walk around and around the cage. The other people had to come and make her stop. Finally the child's original parents heard about it, and they came and showed her scars to the police. There was lots of this going on even when I was young. The Japanese police would beat the parents and say, "Now we let you see how it feels." But some parents began to take their daughters back when they found out about these things. When we adopted my Gim-hua I didn't like her very well—it was my husband who liked her—and so my mother-in-law was afraid that I would be like everybody else and hurt her. I finally told her to stop worrying. If the child was going to be in my family I'd treat her that way. I didn't like it very much, but I just decided, "She's here and so that's it."

In modern Taiwan parents have become very self-conscious about their treatment of adopted daughters, but they still make no pretense of an adopted child being the equal of their own children. Adopted daughters, unless they are the only children of their foster parents, are less likely to go on to middle school than their female classmates. A young woman we knew well spoke to us frankly about her status as an adopted daughter. She was the only adopted child of a couple who had three other children, a girl two years her senior and two younger boys. "I think the reason I was given out as an adopted daughter was because my father died right after I was born. My mother only had two boys and two girls—she shouldn't have given me away. No one here has treated me really badly, but not particularly well either. When a girl is an adopted daughter, no matter how well she is treated, she is always a little lower than a real daughter . . . unless her foster mother has no other children. Usually people won't let adopted daughters go to school very long. They keep them at home to do the housework. No matter how good you are, they say, 'Oh, she's just an adopted daughter.' There are a lot of people now who say even if they starve to death they won't give a daughter away to be adopted. There are very few fathers who treat their daughters as well as my foster father treats my sister. He is always giving her money, and she goes to Taipei at least once a week to 'play.' " When we first met this girl we assumed she was the family servant, so differently was she dressed from her older sister. She told us later that she did not need new clothes and could wear her older sister's castoffs because she did not go out very often. Movies were cheap in the local market town, and she was allowed to go fairly often, but she did not need nice clothes to go there. Her sister, who went to movies only in Taipei, naturally needed nicer clothes. Our observations of the girl's relations with her older sister did nothing to clarify our original misunderstanding of her status in the family. The older girl ordered her around much as she might a servant, and her foster mother gave her complete responsibility for the more burdensome chores in the house.*

We asked a forty-four-year-old woman about her early life as an adopted daughter. She told us, but she got more and more upset as her memories began to flow. The interview ended in tears.

* I have described an adopted daughter in a similar position in Chapter 6 of *The House of Lim.*

Well, you know that until recently people all wanted to exchange their girls for adopted daughters so they could marry them to their sons. People used to come to get the girls as soon as they were born because they were afraid someone else would adopt them. I think I was three months old when I was given away. [My parents gave me away] because they wanted a girl to marry to my older brother. When I was adopted my foster mother had a milk child [i.e., she was a wet nurse] to make money on, so I could only have the milk that was left over. There wasn't enough, so I had to eat rice water and other things. My foster sister tells me how the neighbors used to call her the fifteen-year-old mother because she took care of me like a mother. You know, when a baby doesn't have enough to eat, it cries all the time. My foster mother would get angry and just throw me on the bed. Then my foster sister would take me and heat some powdered milk or rice water to feed me. Everyone says she was very good to me. My foster mother was always beating me. It wasn't that she didn't like me, it was just her temper. She beat me whenever she was angry. Sometimes I'd be sitting doing my homework, and she would grab me and hit me for no reason at all that I knew of. I knew that I was an adopted daughter and had to be very careful. I did my homework and never got into fights. Sometimes she would hit me so much that I would bleed, and I would run away and she would still chase me to beat me more. When my foster sister got married and had a child, I came home right after school and carried the baby because I knew my foster mother couldn't beat me with the baby on my back. I wanted to go to school so much that I got my older sister to enroll me when I was nine years old. Oh, I can still remember the beating I got for that. As soon as I came home from school, I went to work making temple money [a cottage industry]. I can remember looking out the window when I was pasting the money, watching the other kids play. If my foster mother left, of course I would sneak out and play. Naturally, I would forget my work and if my foster mother came back and caught me, I was really in trouble. Really when I think of my childhood, I wonder why my fate was so bad. My foster mother beat me too often and too hard. I was always trembling with fear.

The childhood attitude of adopted daughters toward their "real" parents and natal homes is unusual. "Little daughters-in-law," like adult daughters-in-law, are invited to return to their natal homes at New Year and for such occasions as the marriage of a brother or a funeral. I assumed that these visits would be bittersweet pleasures for children who were given so little in their foster homes, but in fact they seemed to be terrifying occasions. The woman I quoted above told us: "You know it was very strange when I was a child. My foster mother was always beating me, but even so, whenever I heard that someone from my natal family had come to take me home for a visit, I was scared and ran and hid in the toilet. My older brother and my foster mother would all come and try to get me to come out, but I wouldn't come out. At that time it seemed to me that going back to my natal home was just like they were going to cut a piece of meat off my body." "Why were you afraid to go home? Did your foster mother threaten you?" "No, I don't know why it was. I just didn't want to go away. My foster mother beat me and beat me, but if I didn't see her for even a few hours I would cry and run around looking everywhere for her."

A young woman in her twenties told us she had very much the same feelings. "When I was a child I was terrified when someone from my natal family came to take me home. I would hide behind the bed or in the pigpen. Now when I think about it, it seems very strange. I didn't want to go home when I could, but now when I'd like to, my foster parents won't let me." Another woman told us about a daughter she had given away. "Whenever I bring her home to visit, she doesn't want to stay. When I go to get her, she gives me a hateful look and turns her head away. I don't know why this is. Usually at that age they don't understand things. I don't know whether she is mad because I gave her away or what. She just doesn't like me. She plays with her brothers and sisters happily enough, but she doesn't like me. Whenever someone asks her about me, she tells them that I'm not her real mother, but her older sister's mother." If these children had been adopted at the age of four or five, their terror of another abandonment might account for their attitude toward a temporary separation from their foster mothers and foster homes, but most girls are adopted before they are a year old and remember little or nothing about their parents and their adoption. The reaction is obviously a more subtle psychological phenomenon, one that cannot be unrelated to the very different treatment that produces the type of personality considered to be typical of the *sim-pua*—obedient, sullen, uncommunicative.

For both the men's family and the women's uterine family, the *sim-pua* form of marriage had real advantages over other marriage types. The cost of raising a child, often a child who replaced one born to the family, was not comparable to the ruinous expenses of bride price, engagement cakes, and feasts required by the major marriage. When the couple were old enough to marry, their bow to the ancestors need only be acknowledged by a simple family feast. Wealthier families also chose the *sim-pua* form of marriage, but often made it as expensive as the major form by returning the bride to her natal home a few weeks before the wedding and marrying her in with all the pomp usually associated with a wedding. Both wealthy and poor families saw advantages in the *sim-pua* form of marriage beyond those of economy; they valued the safety of having a daughter for a daughter-in-law. No outsider had to be brought into the heart of the family. The family did not need to depend on the word of a go-between and the dubious judgments of relatives about the character, honesty, industry, health, and good nature of the woman who was to spend the rest of her life in their house and take care of them in their old age. By the time a girl adopted in infancy was old enough to be mated with a son, her strong and weak points were well known. If a mother had any serious misgivings about her, she could arrange another marriage for her son; if she was satisfied with the end product of her training, she had an inexpensive daughter-in-law. The girl was not likely to be extravagant unless her adopted parents had taught her to be. She knew the ways of the household and had learned from an early age how to cooperate with her mother-in-law in the various household tasks. She had never been a daughter, so she was unlikely to make unsatisfactory comparisons with a former life style—in fact, her loyalties *were* those of a daughter. She had been trained from childhood to expect the less pleasant half of any task, to be last in line for hand-me-downs, to eat what was left, and to keep one eye on other people's faces. In short, she was trained as a daughter-in-law from infancy and had never passed through the disquieting experience of being a daughter.

When a *sim-pua* was married to her foster brother she did not, as does a girl making a major marriage, suffer a complete severing of ties. Her strongest emotional tie was to her mother–mother-in-law, and that tie was not disrupted; her primary loyalty was to the uterine family of her mother–mother-in-law, and that loyalty was not disrupted. She posed no threat to her mother-in-law's relations with her son because she was unlikely to try to use him. Her mother-in-law's uterine family was *her* family, and when she bore children she was not desperate to make them exclusively hers. She was already living in the most secure setting she had ever known, and she had no desire to use her husband to remove her from it. When she needed help from someone with power in the family, it was likely to be her mother-in-law to whom she appealed. The *sim-pua*'s position in the women's community was like her position in the family, slightly lower than the others. The advantage of being a long-term resident was balanced by the stigma of her adoption, and by the silent sullen behavior that kept most *sim-pua* from becoming forces in the community—until their mothers-in-law died. The community's expectations of a *sim-pua* are both higher and lower than its expectations of a married-in woman. She is looked down on because of her status, but she is expected to be as close emotionally to her mother-in-law as a daughter. Whereas fiery quarrels are expected between mother-in-law and daughter-in-law, a *sim-pua* would be condemned by the women of the village if she and her mother–mother-in-law did not live together in peace.

In the 1930's there was a dramatic change in the rate of adoption in northern Taiwan. From 70 per cent of girls being given in adoption in 1910, the rate dropped to 44 per cent in 1931, and the custom of adopting girls as future daughters-in-law disappeared almost completely. The virtual demise of this form of adoption and marriage was not a matter of parental decision, but the result of filial rebellion. Brothers began to refuse to marry the girls their parents had spent eighteen years raising for them. The cost of raising a child has always been calculated closely by a Taiwanese farmer. If his son refused to marry an adopted daughter, he had wasted eighteen years of child-rearing money, would be required to bring in a bride at great expense anyway, and to compound his frustration, would have to arrange a marriage for his adopted daughter. The *sim-pua* form of marriage ceased to be a safe and inexpensive form of marriage and became an uncertain luxury. Parents stopped matching each of their sons with an adopted daughter. Only adoptions motivated by other needs continued.

What caused this massive rebellion of young Taiwanese

men? In a word, economic independence. In tooling up for the war to come, the Japanese put a great deal into Taiwan's development, and for the first time there were full-time jobs available for men in the new factories. Prior to this there were few sources of employment for a young Taiwanese; he was dependent on his father for his livelihood. Although many sons were sent out as laborers during planting and harvesting, this was not the steady work on which one married and supported a family. The introduction of factories into the economy brought at least the potential of a future independence and wages sufficient to keep a single person alive. With this possibility as a threat and the very real financial contributions sons began to make to the family budget, the young men began to feel that they had rights as well as duties to their families. The first right they claimed was not the freedom to chose their own brides, but simply the freedom to reject a marriage that was repugnant to them. Men did not want to marry their sisters. They were willing for their parents to continue to choose their brides, but they did not wish to marry *sim-pua*. The result was the near-extinction of a custom that had seemed entrenched in the social system. Mothers and mothers-in-law ceased to adopt *sim-pua*. The introduction of a strange daughter-in-law into the bosom of the family was far less threatening than the rebellion and possible loss of an unmarried son, both to the man's family and to the woman's uterine family.

In talking to men and women who rejected the *sim-pua* form of marriage, we found none of them able to express precisely why they felt so strongly about it. Their embarrassment and their vagueness was a response so similar to the response we met when we tried to interview about sex that my husband finally realized its source. When he began to ask the right questions, it became obvious that the marriage "felt" incestuous to them. The boy and girl were raised from infancy to call each other brother and sister; they slept on the same bed, bathed together, were punished for the same misdeeds, and were generally treated as any other brother and sister. During adolescence some gross teasing might have made them avoid each other in the presence of outsiders, but probably no more so than occurs in the usual sex segregation among Taiwanese children. Finally, one New Year they would be "pushed together," a Taiwanese expression describing both the minimal formalities that establish this kind of marriage and the physical action by the parents that is sometimes required to consummate it. The couple were henceforth expected to behave as man and wife, not as brother and sister. Both found the new relationship unsatisfactory at best, and some found it unbearable. The incidence of adultery and semipermanent liaisons outside the family was much higher among men who married their adopted sisters than it was among men who married in the "conventional" way. A man might marry his *sim-pua* and spend enough nights in her bed to father descendants for the family, but he went elsewhere for his sexual satisfaction.

Extramarital relations on the part of men are neither rare nor worthy of more than passing comment in Taiwan, but the sexual straying of a woman is a serious matter. Even so, in a community near Sanhsia, my husband found evidence that at least one-third of the women married to foster brothers had at some time in their lives had sexual relations with another man. (In contrast, only 11 per cent of the women who had married in the conventional way had such gossip whispered about them.) I suspect that some of this promiscuity may actually be extreme filial behavior. *Sim-pua* know, as do all women, that their function in life is to produce descendants for the men's families. If their brother-husbands are not doing their share, their mothers-in-law may make it clear that there are other bed partners, and even provide opportune moments of privacy for the young women. Uterine families also need descendants.

Another statistic from this same district casts a different light on the apparent satisfaction of the senior generations with the *sim-pua* form of marriage. Only 1.2 per cent of the 171 major marriages in the district ended in separation or divorce, whereas 24.2 per cent of the *sim-pua* marriages ended in divorce or separation. Although the marriage of foster siblings may have produced unusually peaceful households, nearly one-fourth of those families were required to arrange a second set of marriages. This high rate of failure should have discouraged parents from raising wives for their sons, but the Taiwanese in fact seemed to be quite unaware of the poor record. No one ever told us that the *sim-pua* marriage was undesirable because it was so prone to disintegrate, and even the officials who record divorces were unaware of the striking divorce rate.

A few determined families, refusing to acknowledge the obvious demise of this custom, have continued to adopt girls as *sim-pua*. The interview below was taken from a young woman in her middle twenties who a few years before had refused to marry her foster brother. Even in 1958 her strong stand was considered unusual, and forty years ago it would have been quite out of the question. In those days women were totally dependent on their families, and the only way they could support themselves was through prostitution. For some women this was preferable to marriage with a foster brother, but in general the kind of upbringing that a *sim-pua* was subjected to did not produce rebels. The young woman in the interview below was less a rebel than her actions suggest. She was employed in an office and for a Taiwanese woman earned an exceptional income. We began the interview by asking her about the very reserved behavior we had noted in the adopted daughter of one of her relatives. She told us, "Females like us who are given away to be adopted daughters are clever. We are always looking around to see what our position is among people, and we can tell just by looking at people's faces whether they like us or not. When I was in school they used to scold me for studying so hard. I liked to study, but they said I was just pretending because I didn't want to take care of my younger brothers. I was really very naughty. I would look at my foster mother's face and if I knew her mood was 'safe' I would say things like, 'I know I'm not supposed to study, and I'm supposed to take care of them because I'm an adopted daughter.' "

We asked her, "Why do you think people give their own daughters away and then adopt another?" She answered quite bitterly:

I don't know, but I guess that it is because they don't want to make their own daughters work for them. So they adopt someone else's daughter to do their work. I used to get so angry with my parents because they gave me away. Even now I sometimes think that my unhappy life is all their fault. If they hadn't given me away I probably would have had a very happy life. I'm sure it wouldn't be like this. I can remember when I was little. My parents and my foster parents were good friends, so my parents often used to come here. I remember once when I was playing in the yard on a mat and I saw my mother coming, I just rolled myself up in the mat and hid. I didn't want to see her.

I also used to get very mad at my foster mother's daughter. In school I did much better than she did. The teacher would give us two pieces of paper, one to practice on and one to turn in. I would always put my name on the first one and hers on the other. I was the last in the row so I collected all the papers. Nobody said I had to help her in school, but I knew I did. If I came home first, my foster mother would look at me and say, "Where is So-lan?" I would go back to school and call her, but then I wouldn't go home for lunch myself. I would just stay at school.

Girls Who Marry Their Brothers

When my foster grandfather's older sister used to come to visit I can remember hearing my foster mother urge her to eat a little of this and a little of that, saying, "You are still a daughter in this family." She never said anything like that to me. Maybe it was because I was quiet and always sat in the corner with my mouth closed, but I still felt, "No one pays any attention to me because I am an adopted daughter."

I used to hate my parents for giving me away. If they had just opened their eyes and looked before they gave me away, it wouldn't have been so bad. If they had given me to people who didn't have any children they would have liked me, but they gave me to a family that didn't need children, just a wife for one of their sons. Now I know that they [her parents] suffered too. After my foster brother finally married, my mother told me how my foster mother kept coming to her and telling her how badly I was behaving and begging her to try to get me to obey them. But there wasn't anything she could do about it. I hated her even more than my foster mother. I could never get used to the idea of having two mothers. I used to think "Everyone else has only one mother, why must I have two mothers?" I knew that she was my real mother, but I forced myself to think that my foster mother was my real mother, not her.

During the Japanese times when we went to see someone off who was going to the army we used to sign scrolls, and I used to just hate to have to sign my name. Everyone could see that I had two surnames. [Adopted daughters often take the surname of their natal family as the second character of their name.] Once I clutched the pencil so hard in my anger that I broke it. I hated writing my name. Even now I don't like anyone to know I'm an adopted daughter. When I graduated from school, I just struck the second character out of my name. If a person finds out that I'm an adopted daughter it makes me mad right away. When people ask if I have a *gua ke* [natal home], I say no. I feel, "I'm not married. How can I have a *gua ke*?" There are lots of people that treat you just a little differently if they know that you are an adopted daughter.

When the young woman was twenty-one, she was told that she and her brother were to marry the following New Year. Although this announcement did not come as a surprise to her, she obviously was not resigned to her fate. Her brother, who assisted in the family fish shop in the local market town, was apparently ready to go through with the marriage. At any rate, he let her bear the blame for rejecting it. She remarked:

At that time I just felt that it was a bad thing to marry him. I didn't know it would turn out like this. Now I am too old to marry. It would be meaningless for me to marry now. Besides, it is nearly impossible. Except for mainlanders, there aren't any men my age who haven't gotten married. When he wanted to marry me I wouldn't do it, so I just can't go marry anyone now. And I certainly can't marry a mainlander because everyone would laugh at me and talk about it. They would say, "No one else wanted her."

My foster father was very angry with me when I refused to marry his son, but there was nothing they could do. I just wouldn't do it, and I wouldn't run away from here either. They couldn't just kick me out because the neighbors would talk. He used to be so angry he wouldn't speak to me, but not anymore. Now he seems to understand and is nice to me.

Everyone here tried very hard to force this marriage. My foster father didn't say anything to me himself, but he sent for my mother to come and try to talk me into it. All the neighbors talked about it too. My foster mother talked and talked, but she couldn't argue very well, and every time I would answer her she couldn't think of what to say next. The neighbors would say something to her, and she would get mad and come back and scold me. I promised her that I would be very filial in every other way, but I just couldn't do this. Then she died just after my brother got married, so I didn't really have much chance to show her how filial I could be.

Even now that I know I will never be able to marry, I am not sorry for what I did. He and his wife get along very well. If I had married him, I'm sure we would have hated each other by now. And if not by now, then we would have in a little while because we never really liked each other very much. Those who make this kind of marriage and like it are very few. In fact, you can say no one likes it. Really, it is meaningless to marry your foster brother. I really think it is meaningless.

One day after I had told the family I wouldn't marry my brother, a girl friend who had married a mainlander invited me to dinner. She also invited my real parents. After dinner my father started scolding me and urging me to change my mind. I didn't much like that girl friend anyway, and now there was my father trying to lose my face and tell everyone that I was a bad person. I was so angry. My hands were like ice, and I nearly fainted. Finally my mother made him stop talking. After my brother was married, I went home for a visit and my father said, "I don't see how you can stand it. I don't see how you cannot be embarrassed. How can you go on living in that house? I thought that by now you would have left." I couldn't say it because he is my father, but I felt like telling him, "How can you think that I might come back here and try to get used to living with all of you? From the time I was a child I hated you for giving me away, so how could I get used to living with you now?" But I didn't dare say that to my parents.

We asked her, "Why did your father say you should be embarrassed to go on living here? What does that mean?" She replied: "After I had refused to marry the brother they had adopted me to marry, there was no more reason for me to be in this house. Besides, my foster mother was the only one who really liked me, and she died. There just wasn't any point to it anymore. But I just couldn't bring myself to go there and live with my real parents. Not even now that I am older and understand it all.

"I don't see how my foster father could try to make me marry my foster brother. When he married his adopted sister, she ran away a few days after they were married and never came back. I'm sure he must remember this, and so I don't see how he could try to make me marry my foster brother. This lady now lives in Taipei and lives very comfortably. The one time I met her she was very embarrassed. After she ran away, she married someone else, and they were very happy."

We asked, "Why do you suppose she didn't run away before she married him?" "I suppose she was better behaved than I am. But then after she was married the more she thought of it, the more meaningless it became, so all she could do was run away. And I think that was the right thing to do."

We asked, "Why do you say it is meaningless to marry your foster brother?" "I don't know. I just couldn't do it. I was shamed by it. At that time I thought to myself, 'It's just that I don't want to marry yet,' but that wasn't the real reason. I think that it was because he was my brother. Marrying your brother! I felt embarrassed about it. I can't even talk to my brother anymore unless I have to. I am shamed by it. Being an adopted daughter is meaningless.

"It is too late for me to marry now. People would laugh. Children are fun, and I can play with other people's children, but I try not to think about getting married. If I found someone and he turned out to be irresponsible, it would be even worse. The more I think about it, the more scared I get, so I just try not to think about it anymore. Lots of people don't get married now. I'll find some way to feed myself when I'm too old to work."

The girl in this interview implies but never quite says that the reason she has not married is because her parents have been unwilling to make any other arrangements for her. She is basically a very conservative woman. She used all of her will to avoid a marriage that was abhorrent to her, but her independence and her confidence were not sufficient to allow her to meet young men and take the responsibility for choosing one who might be a good husband and father. Her conservatism also prevents her from criticizing her foster family for not arranging another marriage for her. She knows that they have fulfilled their only real responsibility to her by arranging one marriage, a marriage that she rejected. It may well be that the reason the family has not made other arrangements is because it does not wish to lose her contribution to the budget, but the inaction might also be blamed on the early death of both her foster mother and her real mother. Although marriages in Taiwan are frankly arranged to maintain the male line of descent, they are dependent on women for their initiation, a pleasant irony unless, like the woman above, you happen to be caught out of cycle in the system. Her unusual position in a "white collar" job also places her outside the influential women's community. She has no way to lay her complaints before it, and has no senior family member there who could bring pressure to bear in her behalf.

There are still a large number of married couples in Taiwan who early in life called each other brother and sister; there are presently very few adopted daughters who are matched with an older brother as a future mate. The *sim-pua* form of marriage is not a custom that is likely to be revived, but it is one of the more interesting strategies human beings have devised to ensure the continuation of their families. If (as many social anthropologists and some Taiwanese farmers say) a strong bond between husband and wife is a major threat to the patrilineal system, the *sim-pua* marriage was surely an excellent safeguard. Given the particular need for solidarity in the women's uterine families, the *sim-pua* marriage provided perfect unity. It gave a woman maximum control over the members of her uterine family. By substituting a daughter for a daughter-in-law, she exchanged an enemy for an ally and removed the major threat to her exclusive ties with her son. The great popularity of the *sim-pua* form of marriage may have had more than a little to do with the fact that women arranged marriages. It is ironic that they both gained the most and suffered the most.

The advantage of a high number of *sim-pua* marriages for the women's community is less certain. Although the presence of a core of women who have grown up together and are related to one another by way of adoption might contribute to the community's solidarity, the presence of numbers of young women who do not have to leave the only family they have ever known and of older women who are not threatened by an outsider's entry into their uterine families might have the opposite effect. What is required is evidence from a community in which the incidence of *sim-pua* marriages is and always has been relatively low, evidence I unfortunately do not possess.

❧ 12 ❧

Girls Who Have No Brothers

Even with the end of the *sim-pua* form of marriage, there is still a large number of young women who do not leave the homes in which they were raised when they marry. These are girls whose mothers bear no sons and whose families must depend on them to provide descendants and an income for the senior generation. A married couple may adopt a daughter or two or even three before they accept their own barrenness and acknowledge that they must adopt a boy if they are to have a son. A couple who can have children, but produce only daughters, avoid this decision until it becomes apparent that the woman is not going to bear any more children. Female adoptions are simple and cheap, but a male adoption is both hard to manage and expensive. Even parents with several sons are not eager to give one in adoption, and when they do, they expect to be well paid. Often parents without sons hesitate to take this expensive step until they are in early middle age, and then, a few years later, they find themselves in the difficult position of needing an adult male to help the aging father work the land or to supply an income if he has become incapacitated. If the adopted son is still a child (or if the family never accumulated sufficient reserves to buy a boy), there is no alternative but to marry a daughter to a man who is willing to enter the family as a son, casting off some part of his rights and duties as a son to his natal family.

There is nothing more abominable, say the Chinese, than an unfilial son, a man who abandons his parents and leaves his ancestors to suffer unknown deprivations in the afterlife. The man who makes an uxorilocal marriage must transfer his loyalties to the parents of his bride, and his obligations are henceforth to their ancestors. By definition, then, no decent man would make an uxorilocal marriage, and it follows that no man who makes an uxorilocal marriage is decent. A careful look at the background of the men who make such marriages usually reveals that they were orphaned at an early age or never had a father or were the youngest of many sons in families that could not afford to feed their other sons let alone provide them with wives. Nonetheless, the tradition remains. No matter what the circumstances, the man who consents to an uxorilocal marriage is not the equal of other men. He may in fact be conscientious, hard-working, filial, and honest, but the neighbors will know that if nothing else is wrong with him, he is the kind of man who does not care about face.

The person most conscious of the inferiority of the man who marries uxorilocally is the woman who is forced to marry him. Adopted daughters resent uxorilocal marriages, but adopted daughters are used to submission and to being given second-best. Real daughters, and in particular girls who have no brothers, are often their parents' darlings and accustomed to the best. If their parents force them into an uxorilocal marriage their resentment is openly expressed. Children bear the majority of the obligations in the parent-child relationship, but to provide children with the best possible mate is a major parental obligation. Doing such a poor job of it, i.e., marrying a daughter to a man who is by definition inferior, is considered by many girls to be a dereliction of duty. In fact, parents who have both a natural-born daughter they are fond of and an adopted daughter they have always treated as a servant usually allow their daughter to marry out of the family and arrange the fragile uxorilocal marriage for the adopted daughter. There are two possible explanations for this. The one most commonly offered is that the parents want to spare their own daughter the hardship of a second-class marriage. But the advantages of having an adopted daughter as a daughter-in-law are well known to families that are contemplating *sim-pua* marriages, and I imagine these advantages are weighed as well by families that must decide which of two daughters will spend the remainder of her days in the home in which she was raised. Either girl would be resentful of such a marriage, but adopted daughters have learned to live with resentment. A good example of the feelings of women who are required to make an uxorilocal marriage is contained in the following interview. The couple had been married for over ten years. "To marry this kind of 'dead man' is to 'want to die.' He married into my family. I didn't want to marry him, but my foster parents insisted. At that time my foster father had lost a lot of money in business, and he wanted someone to marry in quickly who had an income. My husband was a coal miner then and made good money, and so they talked him into marrying into my family. If I could have married the man I wanted to marry I wouldn't be living this poorly now. That man is doing very well now."

Ideally, the man who marries uxorilocally changes his surname to that of his wife, renounces all claim to his children as his own father's descendants, and agrees to behave as a son to his wife's parents and their ancestors. Families that require the total abrogation of other ties usually have difficulty finding a respectable candidate—unless they have obvious wealth that will one day be inherited by the man. If a man is invited to marry a girl who has a younger brother with whom he will have to share the family estate, or even sisters who will be married uxorilocally, he will be reluctant to commit himself so completely to the family. As a result there are several recognized variations in uxorilocal marriages. Parents who simply need financial support until a younger son is old enough to provide for them may arrange for a man to marry into the family without requiring him or his children to take their surname. Often this arrangement also binds him for a minimum period of time and once he has fulfilled his obligation he is free to take his wife to his own family home if he has one or to set up a separate household. Other variations require the man to assign his first child or his first son (or alternate children or sons) the surname of his father-in-law's family and to oblige these children and their descendants to take the responsibility for the tablets of their maternal grandfather's ancestors. Although the limitations of the man's marriage agreement will be known in detail by the neighbors, they will still regard him as "that man who married into his wife's family."

Of the various forms of marriage, the uxorilocal is the most brittle. Few adult men can tolerate the attitude of the family and neighbors and behave with the humility apparently expected of them. They are, in a limited sense, male brides. Just as the bride must be quiet and submissive, watching carefully to anticipate the moods of her parents-in-law, so should the young groom behave. And if the bride is considered a dangerous or at least a suspicious outsider, the groom is seen as an out-and-out threat. The mother keeps up a running criticism of him, which intensifies if she detects any signs of sympathy in her daughter. It is assumed, and with good reason, that the man's only object is to "lure" the family's daughter into running away with him. A young coal miner lasted only two months in an uxorilocal marriage before running off, taking his wife with him. His mother-in-law told of it with real fury. "He was a worthless man who was unwilling to work, and he carried off my daughter even though I treated him very well. After they ran away we looked all through the bamboo groves along the riverbank because we thought they might have jumped into the river. I was so good to him and yet he ran away with my daughter, and so I hated him. I asked the gods to let him be crushed to death in a mining accident. A year later when I heard that his shoulder had been broken in an accident, I was very happy. But then he recovered. So I told a god that if he would let that man be killed I would burn a hundred sticks of incense to him in an open field. Later when my neighbors came and told me that he had been crushed beyond recognition in the mine, I was so happy that I laughed and laughed. That was about ten years ago, and after that my daughter went to live with a peddler. She still lives with him, but I don't know why. He is short and ugly. You would laugh just to look at him." We asked some of the neighbors why the couple had run away, since they were treated well, and were told, "If they were really so good to him, why did they first search the riverbanks when he and his wife disappeared?"

The wife in an uxorilocal marriage finds herself caught between two cultural dictates. She must obey her parents before she marries and her husband after she marries, but when both husband and parents are exercising authority over her simultaneously, the rules are not clear. A young woman we knew in Peihotien, who often took her parents' side in their quarrels with her husband, was censured by at least one of her neighbors. "That woman! She already has two children, but she still sides with her father when he and her husband get into an argument. Where else could one find a woman like that! He married into her family and so her father and mother are always saying things to him, but she always takes their side. It is as though she was just married and she already has two children!" Yet a woman who through her husband is the sole support of her aging parents would be roundly condemned for abandoning them. Her more charitable neighbors might recognize the evil influence of her husband, but the wife would still be held culpable. A young woman who is resentful of her parents for forcing her to make a marriage that is inferior (at least in type) may be less inclined to side with them against her husband. This is particularly true in marriages that have been arranged by the couples themselves. When we discovered that a woman in her late twenties had chosen the man who had married into her family, we asked if her parents had objected. She answered, "How could they? It isn't easy to find a man willing to make this kind of marriage." By submitting to an uxorilocal marriage, this woman felt she had at least earned the right to choose the man for herself.

Young women do not reserve their resentment for the fathers for whose descent line their marriages have been sacrificed. They also blame their mothers, the agents who must reject inquiries from families wanting brides and must do the searching for men willing to marry uxorilocally. Unless the mother can overcome the daughter's bitterness, her uterine family may be destroyed by the arrival of a son-in-law. Even if the young man is not eager to sever his wife's loyalties to her mother, the younger woman may be more inclined to form her own uterine family than a *sim-pua* in similar circumstances, rejecting her mother's uterine group and in effect leaving her alone and isolated. Oddly enough, mothers tend to view their sons-in-law as the major threat (much as they do daughters-in-law in major marriages), ignoring the motives that drove them to found their own uterine families when they first entered their husbands' households.

To be sure, not all uxorilocal marriages create destructive strains in the household. There was one marriage in Peihotien that was repeatedly pointed out to us as an example of what an uxorilocal marriage ought to be.* The mother-in-law was plainly well satisfied:

> When my son-in-law was a child, his mother was going to let us adopt him, but we still hoped to have a son of our own and then we stopped talking about it, and it never got settled. When the man his mother was living with died, she lived with Cui-bok [a distant male relative of the speaker] because neither of them had a husband or a wife. Then when she died, nobody wanted Cin-chiong so he just stayed on with Cui-bok. Cui-bok's daughter complained every time she had to wash Cin-chiong's clothes and wouldn't let him go to school beyond the sixth grade. He went out to work in the mines and because he was such a good boy, the mine operator trusted him and gave him better jobs. Later, one of our neighbors came and asked me if I wanted to let my daughter marry out or what. I said, "Of course not." She was my only adopted daughter so how could I let her marry out of the family. I told her [the neighbor] she could look around and see if she could find someone to marry in if she wanted, but not to think about anybody who wouldn't. Without even telling me she went and asked my daughter what she thought of Cin-chiong. My daughter thought well enough of the match that she came and talked to me about it.

> We couldn't decide whether we wanted him or not. You know, if a boy can make money himself, he isn't willing to marry into a girl's family, so we looked him over carefully. At that time he really was not too hard-working, so we were afraid of how he might turn out later. I went to the temple to ask the god about it, and the god said it was all right. I took a fortune paper but I forgot to ask the priest what it meant. Everyone at home looked at it and said it looked all right, but nobody was sure. My husband said, "Oh, you stupid woman. Why didn't you ask?" So the next day I went back, and the priest said, "If you are going

---

* This is the marriage of Ong Thuan-cong's adopted daughter mentioned in Chapter 2.

197

to have someone marry out of your family it is very good." And then I told him we were going to have someone marry into the family, and he said that was even better. So that was it.

After he was married, Cin-chiong helped his wife a lot. If he came home from work and she was busy cooking, he would help her by feeding the pigs. [She laughed at this, clearly finding it a little funny for a man to help his wife with her chores.] If he was tired when he came home, he would take a nap and then go out to work in the fields. If he wasn't tired he would go right to work. We never have had to tell him. Really, he works very hard. He's not bad at all, but then when you think that all of these things are going to belong to him, he would be pretty stupid not to work to keep them. It's my daughter that is beginning to be bad. Before she was married, she was a very good girl, and I liked her very much. You never had to ask her twice to do something. She did it as soon as you told her, but now she won't mind at all.

Except for the foster mother's complaints about her daughter, complaints that probably reflect her barely conscious recognition of the younger woman's shifting loyalty to her husband and her new uterine family, this is a peaceful household that has solved a very serious problem. For all practical purposes, the parents now have a son who is industriously working their land as well as providing a cash income. Besides supporting them, he has given them two grandsons and two granddaughters.

Since the uxorilocal marriage is less than desirable from the man's point of view, it is surprising that many quite decent men are willing to marry into a family. Cin-chiong, the young man discussed above, could have had no misgivings, for he had no parents to support and no surname to abandon. Still, his income would have allowed him to take a wife and set up a modest household of his own. In modern Taiwan this seems to be the goal of some young couples chafing under the rule of the husband's parents, but for a number of young men, this alternative is less attractive than occupying a lowly status in an established family. To a Chinese, the family does not mean just his wife and unmarried children. It means a miscellany of relatives, a place they all come back to on feast days, the sounds of a baby crying, kids arguing, and women gossiping, a collection of farm animals, a family altar, neighbors whose great-grandparents knew his great-grandparents, and a place in the community that is his, for all time. Many young men who never knew this family life as children or lost it as adults are willing to accept a father-in-law's family as a substitute. These roots are clearly what many mainlanders who marry into their wives' families are searching for. Of course, a young man from a poor family may well be considering the more mundane side of an uxorilocal marriage. He gets a bride without the extravagant cost of a Taiwanese wedding, and if the family has any property, he may become the heir. Even if the family is not propertied or has insufficient land for its needs, there is security in marrying into an established family. If he loses his job, the family roof will still be over his head. Until he finds work the family can make do on vegetables from the family garden and credit at the village store. For a young man on his own, with no family at all, a week without an income could mean no roof and no food.

It is, not surprisingly, this point—the security gained in such marriages—that most parents fear is uppermost in the mind of any man willing to marry into their family. If the man's earning capacity is one of the primary reasons he is brought into the family, his loss of work is considered a disaster. Indeed, it may even be considered treachery. A Peihotien couple married their daughter, a prostitute with three illegitimate children, to an elderly goldsmith who worked in a shop in Wanhua. Six or seven years later, the old man got into a fuss of some sort with his employer and quit. The woman's family was furious, but he ignored their caustic comments, took a week's vacation, and then went off to look for work in another shop. His age and his former employer made the search far more difficult than he had expected. After six months he still had not found a job, and his wife's family were ruthless in their comments about him. By the time the year was out, the quarreling within the family (a large one with the wife's father's brother living in the same compound) was a daily source of gossip for the neighbors. Since the elderly son-in-law was not fulfilling his obligations to the family, he was expected to be very humble, watching other people's faces and trying to be as helpful as possible. This humility was totally beyond him. Finally, the family talked him into becoming a peddler. His mother-in-law, a woman only a few years his senior, told us, "First he was going to sell sweet-rice and so I bought all the things, but he brought it all home every night. Then he said he would try to sell pig's blood, so I borrowed some money and bought all that. He worked for one day and brought all that home. Then he tried to sell balloons and candy and toys, but he couldn't sell a thing. He would just sit there like a dead man. He didn't call out to customers, and one look at his face would convince people they didn't want to buy anything from him. He tried to buy junk, too, but just lost us more money. Finally, his wife told him he would just have to go down to the river with her and collect rocks for the construction companies. He wouldn't even try that. He said it was too hard for a man his age. So then he just sat at home and told the rest of us what to do. This kind of man! He has to lean on his wife to make money to feed him. What use is he? Can you still call this a man?" One morning the old fellow gathered up his two daughters and when all the family was out, he walked away. When he was discovered missing, there was no great outcry. Within a week his wife went to Taipei to work—as a cook, according to her parents. A few months later a neighbor told us, "Well, if she is a cook, she cooks all night. She is going to have a baby in a few months."

There were other families in Peihotien that had equally dreary histories of driving out married-in sons-in-law when their earning capacity failed. A family's chance of finding a truly respectable, hard-working young man after an initial failure in an uxorilocal marriage is very slim. As often as not, the parents merely encourage their daughter to find a man willing to live with them and provide some income with no discussion of other obligations. There were several women in Peihotien whose "marriages" turned out to be more or less temporary alliances not even noted in the Household Registration Office. A very respectable middle-aged woman, whose two married sons had blessed her with several grandsons, told us that her husband died when he was quite young. When we discovered that her two sons were listed as illegitimate in the household registers, we began to question some of her older neighbors. She was, we were told, the only child of her parents to survive to adulthood. The parents were hopelessly poor, and when they could find no one willing to marry into their family, they simply encouraged the girl to provide them with descendants. She never worked as a prostitute, the usual fate of girls in such families, but she had had several lovers, all of whose progeny were given her father's surname. This technique for ensuring a descent line is not uncommon in Taiwan. A young woman whose husband dies before she has borne any sons may be urged by his parents to stay with them. Feeble attempts may be made to find a man to marry in, and if that fails, the family simply lets nature work things out. Virtuous widows among poor farm families were filial widows who stayed with their parents-in-law. Their sex life was not relevant.

Even in a country as concerned with descent as China, there sometimes is a vagueness about just what constitutes a marriage. There was considerable disagreement among our neighbors in Peihotien over whether another neighbor, Lim So-cu, had or had not been married. We were told:

So-cu was married to a man who still lives in Wanhua. They met each other there because she used to work there. Her three children are all his. He told me his side of it. He said he was interested in another girl and once at the factory [where they all worked] he whistled to attract her attention, but So-cu turned around instead. That was the beginning of their friendship. He was going to marry her, and he brought all the engagement cakes. I think So-cu was already pregnant by then because her mother only asked for NT $1,200 for the bride price. The problem was that So-cu was adopted to marry her foster brother and was registered with the police as his wife. Someone told him that he could get some money too if she married, and so the night before the engagement he went and asked the boy to give him NT $1,200 too. The next day when the boy came with the cakes he demanded the money. The boy was angry and refused. He just sold all the engagement cakes right here in the village and very cheaply at that. Everyone had a good time! After that he came and took So-cu to live with his family for a few months, but she didn't like her mother-in-law and came back here frequently. All three of her children were born here and not at his house. The last time she came home, she didn't return.

So-cu lived with her widowed mother for a few years, picking up a few dollars here and there by weeding for local farmers and gathering rocks in the riverbed for a construction company. While working for the construction company she met a man who was attracted to her, and he has been living with her and her mother for the last several years, contributing to the household expenses, disciplining the children, and chatting with the neighbors in the evening like any other village husband.

In Taiwan it is rare for a woman not to marry in some form

or another. In 1958 in Peihotien there were no older women who had not had a mate at least long enough to provide themselves with children, and there were only three women of marriageable age who seemed likely not to marry. One was the adopted daughter whose long interview was quoted in the last chapter. Another was the adopted daughter of the Ong family who held the well-paid job in a bank. In the Ong girl's case, the parents refused to consider a marriage out of the family since they had only one other child, an adopted son, who was not yet earning much of an income. The adopted daughter for her part refused to submit to an uxorilocal marriage, which she considered beneath her; her income could match and probably exceed that of any man who might consider such a marriage, except for a mainlander, who was out of the question for other reasons. Although the rules may have changed now, in 1958 a woman was not allowed to continue in certain positions in the private banks in Taiwan after marriage, apparently in the fear that a husband might undermine her honesty. At any rate, the rule was sufficient to make this woman's rejection of an uxorilocal marriage stick. In her late twenties she adopted a girl, and when we left the village she was negotiating to adopt a son. She had provided her foster parents with descendants, forestalling any criticism on that score, and had provided herself with a uterine family.

The only other woman in Peihotien who clearly was not going to marry was a deaf-mute. She was an intelligent woman, but no effort had been made to educate her, and she spent her days working in the fields. As long as her parents are alive, she can be assured of a home and food, but after their death life may become even more difficult for her. The life of a woman who does not marry and does not provide herself with descendants is pathetic when she is too old to sell her labor or her body to earn a bowl of rice. Brothers have mixed feelings about adult sisters, particularly since increased literacy has led some to the information that by law a daughter has a right to claim an equal share in her father's estate (a law that is at present almost totally ignored in the countryside). And brothers' sons are even less inclined to feel that they have any responsibility for a feeble maiden aunt. It is for this reason, if no other, that women marry, or, as in the case of the woman banker discussed above, provide themselves in some way with a family and descendants.

From the vantage of the men's families, uxorilocal marriages are an emergency measure, a way of bridging a gap in the line of descent where there is no son. But in depending on a woman to carry them across a generation, they are introducing a flaw that may be fatal to the line of descent. As we have seen in earlier chapters, most girls consider themselves irrelevant to their father's family and are not imbued from their earliest years with a sense of its importance. They spend their formative years with women and grow up with the knowledge that it is what they themselves can create, the uterine family, that is important to their future. If a girl is then forced to make an uxorilocal marriage, who is to teach her sons the mystery and the power of an unbroken chain of ancestors? Her husband is going to be ambivalent at best about his father-in-law's line of descent, and, as we have seen, he may not be a very permanent member of the household in any event. If the grandfather has the good fortune to live long, he may be able to instill in his young grandsons the necessary values, but if he does not, the boys may grow up without conflicting loyalties. They will have strong personal loyalties to their mother and the uterine family, but only a vague cultural knowledge of their allegiance to a line of descent.

ᴥ 13 ᴥ

Filial Daughters

Prostitutes are probably more realistic than most women in Taiwan about the necessity of providing for their old age. Most prostitutes marry at some point in their lives, but quite often the union is neither a conventional marriage nor a stable one. We asked a neighbor in Peihotien if she thought it was harder to find husbands for girls who do this kind of work. She answered, "Oh, they meet someone at work who they like and then they marry him." We asked if the man's family might not object. "Most families don't like to have that kind of girl marry in, so it is a lot more difficult if the man has a family. But some people say that they would rather marry a prostitute [because she knows how difficult that way of earning a living can be] than to have your wife run away and become one after you marry her. Many of the women who do this kind of work become rich men's concubines later on." I rather doubt that "many" of the women who are prostitutes become concubines of rich men in later life, but a good many do meet lonely men without families who frequent wineshops and brothels for companionship. Although not wealthy, they may have sufficient means to pay a reduced version of the girl's wages to her family and in a sense "buy her out." Other lonely men are willing to make an uxorilocal marriage, thereby freeing their wives from the brothels and providing themselves with a home. These are often the most fragile of all uxorilocal marriages because the parents are very conscious of an alternative income if the man should for some reason fail to provide. Parents also worry about evidence of their daughter's emotional attachment to the man, since he could deprive them completely of both incomes by talking her into leaving them. Even parents who wish only the best for their daughter try to sabotage any liaison that might threaten their relations with her. The marriages of prostitutes that seem to fare best are those made by women who have fulfilled their obligations to their parents and can marry without divided loyalties. We knew some thoroughly respected and respectable farmwives who had supported destitute parents and younger siblings for some period of time in the only occupation open to them. We also met a pillar of Sanhsia society, the mother of a schoolteacher, whose distant relative revealed in an unguarded moment some facts about her early years in the southern part of the island. Hers was a long and honorable marriage.

Unless a prostitute for one reason or another is convinced that she is only serving a term in that profession and will return to normal life in a few years, she will usually adopt a daughter two or three years after she begins to work. In fact, the adoption of a little girl is often a sign the woman is resigned to a different life style from that of her peers in the villages. She may later bear illegitimate children or adopt another girl. I doubt if any prostitute ever gives up hope of marrying and living a conventional life, but once she has accepted her profession as part of her identity and not just something imposed on her, she sets about forming a uterine family. One is tempted to accept at face value the assertion that prostitutes adopt little girls simply to have someone to support them when they are too old to work. This is true, to be sure, but most of the retired prostitutes among our neighbors in Peihotien had more than one child. They and their neighbors knew that the more children they had, the less likely they were to find a man willing to take responsibility for their ménage. A prostitute is driven by much the same needs as her respectably married sisters to form a uterine family. She feels very much alone, even though she may be the supporting member of her natal family, and she wants to build her own uterine circle of financial and emotional security.

With the advent of dancehalls, increased independence, and a growing youth culture, some Taiwanese girls today are being attracted by the outwardly glamorous life of a successful prostitute as an alternative to the drab life of the villages. But the generation of women who were working as prostitutes in the late 1950's entered the profession out of financial necessity, either their own or their parents'. Some, like the girl I describe in Chapter 8 of *The House of Lim*, were raised by their prostitute mothers to support them after their own looks faded to the point where they were unemployable. These girls usually are sent to work at the first sign of physical maturity, often in their early teens. Other women are forced or encouraged to enter or re-enter the profession when an uxorilocal marriage fails. It is significant that in Peihotien in 1959, of the twenty-eight women who were or had at one time been prostitutes, twenty were adopted daughters and the other eight girls who had no older brothers capable of supporting their parents. Parents in desperate need of an income might try for an uxorilocal marriage, but failing that, the only recourse is to have their daughters earn the most money possible, which almost inevitably means working as a prostitute. The girl's beauty determines where she works and her charm how much she is paid; a gifted girl contributes, for a few years at least, far more money than most sons-in-law.

Although Taiwanese country people are very straitlaced when it comes to discussing the physical act of sex, they have quite a tolerant view of the woman who uses prostitution to support her parents. They have seen even their most respected neighbors and relatives fall on such hard times that they are forced to send their girls to work. As long as the daughter on her days home behaves herself as any other village girl and, more specifically, neither practices her trade nor brings her customers into the village, she is not treated with the derision she could expect in the West. A family who had had a long series of misfortunes came to live briefly in Peihotien to be near relatives. One night the daughter, who was working in a brothel in Wanhua, came home in the company of a village husband. Apparently the next morning her mother was informed, and that evening the girl was severely scolded. Her mother finished with a brief lecture on propriety. "We are just living here temporarily, but we cannot go around as we please. We have to be friends with all the people here. This man has a home and children, and so he cannot afford to run around. It doesn't matter whether he has money in his pocket or not. We can only be his friend. We cannot threaten his home. You have to remember that you cannot damage people's relations with other people in the place where you live."

In a village setting, most people are aware of their neighbors' problems—economic and social. They are also aware of all the alternatives available to them. They could hardly condemn a girl who obeys her parents and sacrifices her own opportunity for a normal life by becoming a prostitute. If she behaves herself in the village, they tend to regard her as a particularly filial young woman who has paid her debt to her parents more completely than other young women. Her parents are likely to find village opinion against them if they press further demands on the girl. One family in Peihotien was pronounced guilty of greed by the village women, and the frankly impolite, unfilial behavior of the couple's daughters was considered just punishment. The following interview is typical of the village attitude toward the parents.

When the girl was fourteen years old her father made her go to work as a prostitute. He didn't like to work himself, and his wife worked very hard to make a living by raising vegetables and gathering rocks for the construction company. He made the oldest girl go to work as a prostitute because the family was large and very poor and because the sons were all too young to work. For a while she cried every time she came home. Later, she gained a reputation as the most beautiful girl in Peitou. During this time the family lived very well, with new clothes and plenty to eat. Then, because one girl made so much money, the mother decided to send the adopted daughter when she got old enough. She didn't want to go either, but when she refused the family was very angry and wouldn't talk to her. Finally the older sister said, "I'm a real daughter of this family, and I went to work. You are only an adopted daughter, so why can't you come to work?" The mother later told everyone that the girl wanted to go to work when she saw how much money her sister could make, but we all knew that this wasn't true. That second girl now has an illegitimate child, and she never has been able to make much money. After a while the older girl found a man who wanted to marry her, but her mother was a very stupid, selfish woman and wouldn't let her marry even then. Now the old woman is poor and unhappy, and it is all her own fault. After the older girl bore her first child she began to lose her looks and earned less and less money every year. She had a child every year after that, until now she has four children. She moved away from the Peitou hotels after her first child was born because she was embarrassed about how she had changed. Now she is a very emotional person, crying suddenly without reason. She often vomits blood, and the doctor has told her that she must quit this work, but she won't. Her mother told her she could get married now, but she said, "No, I'll work until I'm too ugly and then you can work and support me." Really, that mother has to work very hard now to cook and clean for all those children, and the girls treat her just like a servant. That old lady is very miserable now because of her own selfishness.

Many families attempt to conceal the fact that they have sent a girl out to work as a prostitute. The most common explanation of her peculiar hours is that she is working as a cook or on the night shift in a factory. For the older and less attractive women the hours may not be that much of a problem, since the brothels of the lower-class districts have much of their trade during the daylight hours. But sooner or later, the girl is greeted on the street by a customer or in some other way is pointed out, and the family accepts the disclosure as gracefully as possible. We heard the following conversation between two neighbors about a third. "Do you think she is a prostitute?" "I know she is. She wasn't married to that man. She just lived with him for a while. She started back to work again two weeks ago." "Why did she go back to work?" "Her father and mother both gamble a lot, and the baby needs powdered milk, so she has to work. We found out about it from the soldiers who were hauling rock from the riverbed. Some of them had just come from Matsu and recognized her as having worked there for a month. That was the month she told us she went to visit her husband's family." "They aren't that poor. Why did they send her out to work?" "Her father was in jail for a long time, and her mother was too old to go out to work, so they sent her. I thought she was pretty young to be a cook, and I was right."

In 1960 there were three girls in Peihotien who said that they had become prostitutes by their own choice, but a look at their backgrounds makes this doubtful in two of the cases. Nonetheless, there are girls who use the brothels to escape from a marriage they find intolerable, to commit a form of suicide after an unhappy love affair, or even to satisfy the odd urge toward self-destruction that sentimental girls label filial piety. When we asked a neighbor woman why she thought one of these girls had gone to work as a prostitute, she told us, "Last year she wanted to marry Chi-kim, but her mother said that the fortuneteller told her she wasn't supposed to get married until she was twenty-two or something like that. Chi-kim wanted to go ahead with the engagement, but when the mother said something, they stopped talking about it, and later Lian-hua went out to work as a prostitute. She says she wanted to go herself, but it certainly isn't a very good place she is working in. It's an army brothel, and she gets a hundred men a day. There are too many soldiers and not enough girls, so they have to sell tickets and make them stand in line. The soldiers just walk in and then walk out. That is really very hard on a girl who is just starting this kind of work. She is really very brave."

Another village girl's entry into prostitution was explained to us as follows: "It was like this. She was about to be engaged to a boy in Tapu, and she was working in the river gathering rocks for construction companies to make money for her dowry. She met a young mainlander down there who had the same surname, and he said he would call her mother 'mother' also. He came to the house to talk to her family sometimes after work. Later, some people said she 'did things' with this young man, and somebody told her fiancé's family, and they said they didn't want some old thing that a mainlander had thrown away. They called off the engagement, and the girl said she would never find a decent husband now, so she might just as well 'do it,' since everybody said she had anyway. She makes pretty good money and has nice clothes, but she gives most of the money to her parents. She shouldn't do this work too long. If she just works for two or three years and then gets married, it will be all right."

One very attractive young woman, who says quite frankly that she was jealous of the good clothes and fun her girl friend had as a prostitute, got a job in the same brothel. Her working conditions sound considerably more attractive than those of the girls described above.

Our manager is very kind to us. When customers come in, she tells us how to treat them and so forth. She is forty now and has worked at this since she was sixteen, so she can tell just by looking at the men who come in how to handle them. Her family was very poor, and the wages she made as a laborer weren't enough to support them, so she became a prostitute. When her brother was old enough to support the family, she got married. Her husband was a *lo mua* [hoodlum], and she soon left him. She went back to work, and then she married a mainlander. They don't live together anymore. No other brothel makes as much money as hers does. She owns two houses and a truck. She is the only one there I am afraid of. When she is out and we don't have any guests, we play and yell and have a fine time, but when she comes home, we all sit very quietly. We say among ourselves, "The Mother Tiger is back." She really treats us like her own daughters though and doesn't scold us, but you can tell by her face what not to do. I'm a good girl there. When I'm home, I can't stay in the house for ten minutes without going to see what the neighbors are doing, but when I'm there I never like to go out with the other girls. They often go to watch the gamblers, but I don't like to. They always tease me about being such a "good" girl. Really, I'm afraid to go out because I might meet customers, and they stop and talk. It always embarrasses me. They want to know where I live, and I always tell them I come from the south for fear they will come here. I'm afraid to walk around in Tapu, too, because I'm afraid some of the soldiers there might know me. I don't want to talk to them in public with everyone watching.

In modern Taiwan there are new institutions and new social currents that bring country girls into Taipei, usually against their parents' wishes, to exist on the borderline between prostitution and a frivolous life. To work in a dancehall one need not be a prostitute, only pretty and a good dancer with a penchant for pretty clothes. To some flighty young girls this is a far more attractive job than a twelve-hour shift in a factory, and it is usually better paying. But many of the men who come to dancehalls are also looking for a girl to take to dinner and then to a hotel. Most dancehalls organize the girls in small groups assigned to a manager who is responsible to the hall. The girls' time is calculated in fifteen-minute units, and they get roughly half of what the guest pays the manager. The prices in one large dancehall in Taipei in 1970 were NT $21 per fifteen minutes in the afternoon and early evening, and NT $39 per unit after 8:30 P.M. If a man wishes to take a girl out of the hall for the evening, he must pay in advance for all the time units that will be used up while she is out. Even though old customers may be able to negotiate reduced rates for long periods, this unit system still makes a very expensive evening's entertainment when the cost of a meal, perhaps the expense of a nightclub, and the rent of a hotel room are added in. Although the dancehall management ostensibly puts no pressure on the girls to accept dinner and hotel invitations, it must soon become obvious to them that even the most attractive girl cannot fill each period of her workday unless she accepts a dinner invitation and eventually a hotel invitation. Moreover, they are undoubtedly influenced by the social pressure of others who do, the excited chatter of girl friends who have seen the newest shows with customers, and the growing realization that their neighbors and family assume they are sleeping with their dancing partners anyway. Apparently, many girls are firmly convinced that they will meet a wealthy young man who will fall in love with them at first dance and marry them respectably into a city family far, far from the drudgery of a country farmhouse. It happens often enough, I suppose, to keep rebellious girls trooping into the city in search of the escape promised in the movies. Unfortunately, for most girls the escape to the dancehall becomes just the first step to prostitution, an old institution that has changed very little and offers no more future than it ever did. In fact, now that so many girls are coming to it by the same route as women in the West, modern prostitutes may find themselves in an even less enviable position than their forebears. In China, a girl who becomes a prostitute to support her parents is one thing, but a girl who becomes a prostitute to defy her parents is quite another.

❧ 14 ❧

The Rewards of Old Age

The Chinese believe that a man must behave respectfully toward anyone who is even a few years older than himself, and that aged members of a senior generation must be treated with near-reverence. One of a son's major obligations in life is to see that his parents have as comfortable and happy an old age as he can provide. Nonetheless, a woman learns not to depend on what "ought" to happen and, as we have seen, begins to prepare for her old age almost from the day her first son is born by devoting much of her emotional energy to the task of tying him firmly to her. The prostitute adopting a daughter is expressing the same anxiety as the respectably married woman defending her young sons against imaginary threats. We overheard a neighbor gently chiding a young widow for depriving herself so that her children could have some not entirely necessary item for school. She answered, "I don't care about myself. If I don't eat well, it doesn't matter. I just want my children to do well, so that they can take care of me when I am old."

An old lady we knew in Peihotien spent so many years worrying about the various pitfalls of old age (even though she had three sons) that she could not break the habit even when she was clearly *in* old age. She often complained to her friends about the fact that her sons had not yet gotten around to finding a permanent burial site for their father's bones.* A neighbor suggested one day that she take her own money and offer to build the grave in an attempt to shame her sons. She answered, "That is all very well, but what if they take it and use it all? Then there won't be any left for when my eyes finally close. Before my son built the new house I asked him to go buy me a coffin so that if I should die he wouldn't have to run out and buy just any old one. He said, 'You old woman! Why are you always thinking about these useless things. If you must buy a coffin, buy it yourself!' " The neighbor said, "He is right. You worry too much! Have you ever seen a person who died whose body was just left to lie there and rot? When A-thou died she didn't have a dollar, but she had a good enough funeral, didn't she? When your two eyes really close, your sons will spend the money, and they may even make some, too.† You should forget about your funeral and enjoy your money now. Do you really think they will keep it for six years after you die to build a pretty grave? No. They will just divide it three ways and spend it. I would use all that money for meat and good things to eat. What is the use of keeping it?" "I don't have that much left, just enough for my funeral. That's all." "Look at Siu-lian. She was really poor, but when she died those daughters of hers got money from somewhere and gave her a really big funeral. So what are you worrying about? You have sons. If they can stand to let you sit in the hall and rot, then you shouldn't worry about it. You will be dead. Hurry up and spend your money and

* Chinese practice what anthropologists call double-burial. The body is buried in a shallow grave for a number of years, after which the coffin is opened and the bones removed and placed in a jar. This urn is then placed in a permanent and more elaborate grave, the site having been chosen by a geomancer to bring good fortune to all the family members.
† It is a common notion among those who have not had a funeral in the family recently that the gifts of money from relatives can bring a profit. Gifts do help but never to the point of profit.

enjoy yourself. If you die and they do spend all your money to pay for a big funeral, people will just say, 'Oh, what good sons they are. What a fine funeral they gave for her.' They won't say that it was you who paid for it. If it were me, I'd spend every cent now, and if they could stand to just roll me up in a mat, that would be their worry." "Oh, no, I can't do that. What if I spent all my money and then didn't die for a long time? What then?"

Although anxieties about old age are nearly always expressed in economic terms, there is another fear a middle-aged woman finds harder to express but nonetheless real. She fears she may be returned to the loneliness that marked her early years of married life, to that desolate period when she was firmly rejected by her natal family and not yet accepted by her husband's family. Suppose that by the time she is old and helpless her sons have divided the family property and as a result the uterine family is divided. What has become, then, of the core of security she worked so hard to build? There is a presumption that the eldest son will take responsibility for his aging parents, and for this reason he is given a larger share of the family estate when it is divided. But what if there is no estate or, worse yet, what if her eldest son's wife has managed to alienate her son from her? Some old women are confident of their sons and never experience these fears; others find them groundless. But there are a few pathetic old people in every community who spend their final years being shuffled from one household to another. In a family council each son may agree to take the aged parent(s) for a month or six weeks at a time, with the result that they are constantly moved from one son to the next. If there is a family home to inherit, the sons live in separate apartments in the same house, and the parents take their meals with one or another on a loose schedule; but more often, when the eldest son does not take full responsibility, there is no estate and no family home. The brothers may even live in different towns, and the old folks must move bag and baggage to new localities to pass their last years without the support of familiar faces and a friendly landscape. For an old man, being bundled from family to family is at least a new if bitter experience, but for his wife, it is almost full circle—a return to belonging nowhere.

Some village women become so anxious about their future that they never learn to trust their sons' wives. One woman and her daughter-in-law were famous in the village for the lengths to which each would go to check the other. The old father, who had long ago resigned his headship of the family, was more disgusted with his wife than with his daughter-in-law. One day when we were sitting on some benches near the family's house, the old lady came out in the yard to declaim to the community the most recent of her daughter-in-law's failures. This technique is commonly employed by older people to humiliate a family member they consider incorrigible. "That woman [her daughter-in-law] isn't even going to *pai-pai* [give offerings of food and incense] on the grandfather's death day! She is just going to *pai-pai* to them all on the ninth day of the ninth month [the day when there is a general *pai-pai* for all ancestors, in particular those who may have been neglected on their own death days]. She won't *pai-pai* to them, so I guess they will just have to come back to see her [i.e., the ancestors will send sickness or some other misfortune to indicate their dissatisfaction]." The old lady's husband, who was sitting with us enjoying a bit of winter sunshine, was indignant. "Oh, this old woman. Why does she always have to be scolding at the girl? What does it matter if she does do them all together, as long as she does them? She forgot to buy meat yesterday and today is a meatless day, so what can she do? She already told me she would buy fish and other things, but the old lady didn't see any pork, so she makes all this fuss. What kind of a parent is this? She isn't in charge of the family anymore so it is not her worry." He grumbled off to explain to his wife and try to quiet her before the incident went any further. A neighbor added some notes to the sorry relations between the old woman and her daughter-in-law. "The old lady refuses to eat her daughter-in-law's food and cooks in her room, making a sooty mess out of everything. She claims the daughter-in-law even marks the wood to see how much she uses. To get around her she used some sticks the old man had bought to build a fence. They were really green and filled the house with smoke. And then she is always saying her daughter-in-law won't let her use the water the children carry from the well. The problem there is that the old lady just grabs any old dirty thing handy to dip the water out with, so the daughter-in-law keeps an eye on her to make her use the dipper. One worries that the other is always checking up on her, and the other is always worried that someone is going to mess things up. Eight ounces and a half a catty [i.e., six of one and half a dozen of the other]! The old lady does everything now like she is sneaking, and so naturally the younger one gets suspicious. Really, it is so different now. The mother-in-law seems to be afraid of her daughter-in-law instead of the other way around like it used to be. She doesn't dare scold her to her face anymore, but she scolds her behind her back. It is really her own fault. She doesn't act like a parent anymore, and she was too mean before."

Another old couple we knew in Peihotien live alone except on weekends, when their unmarried children return from the family shoe shop in Taipei. Their loneliness is of their own choosing. Their eldest son is married to a short-tempered woman who is hated by her husband's siblings and who has not always behaved toward her husband's parents as a daughter-in-law should. To avoid the kind of acrimony that dominates the family described in the last paragraph, the old people have chosen to stay in the village, in effect, though not in fact, dividing the household. Both husband and wife are in their late sixties, are apparently in good health, and are very active in village affairs and religious activities. Their unmasked respect and regard for each other make them an unusual couple. Perhaps it is because of this happy relationship that the mother feels so unthreatened by her daughter-in-law's separate household in the city. The old lady told us,

My son always says that we ought to all live together so that we can save some money and reinvest it in the shop. But I know his wife's temperament. She has been in the family for eighteen years, and I have never scolded her, but she often for no reason at all pulls a long face, as though she smelled something bad. I remember when she was first married and came here to live. At that time our neighbor had just married in a daughter-in-law. My daughter-in-law criticized her, saying that her left hand must be crippled because she always ate without picking up her bowl. My son said to her, "You don't know how you look, so how can you laugh at others?" I only added that I didn't think the girl's hand was crippled because I had seen her getting water at the well. I said, "The reason she eats that way is probably because her parents didn't teach her the proper way to hold her bowl. The way you eat, putting one mouthful into your mouth before you have swallowed the last, is not very good to see either. When we eat we ought to eat slowly, swallowing what we have in our mouths before we put in the next mouthful. If we eat like this, people will not laugh at us and say we eat as though we were afraid someone was going to steal our food." No sooner had I finished saying this than she turned blue, jumped up, and said, "You are right. The way I do things is always very hard to look at. Why was it that my parents didn't know enough to teach me? Why did they let me marry into your family where you all laugh at me?" After that she didn't speak to me for ten days. Her husband knew that she wasn't talking to me, but he only said, "Her temperament is the same as her mother's." Well, her temperament hasn't changed. If it weren't for this, we might go to live with them. Their father could help with the store, and I could cook and take care of the children. Having someone in your own family take care of the house is better than having a servant. We could all rest quietly then, not having to worry about some of us being in one place and some in another. We should live together in happiness. But her temperament hasn't changed, and my husband says he would rather stay here and work his fields than go there where he wouldn't have enough to do.

For many women, the last two decades of life are just as they hoped, peaceful years of decreasing responsibilities and increasing leisure time. Household management and many of the chores have been handed to the daughters-in-law. Child care, instead of being a burden among other burdens, is a pleasure, since grandchildren need only to be loved, not trained. Grandmothers are expected to interfere in punishments if they consider them too severe, or undeserved, or if the child cries pitifully. Most grandmothers seem to have very short memories of their own disciplinary techniques and tend to think of their daughters-in-law as extraordinarily harsh. A lively old lady told us with outrage, "My eldest adopted daughter will tell you I only beat her once, and that is when she lost NT $200, and I didn't even hit my second daughter very often—but my son's wife! She is always hitting the children. Before she even tells them what they did wrong, she hits them. I scolded my children first, then I told them why they shouldn't do whatever it was. I didn't hit them all the time. But this one!" The old lady's daughter-in-law, a harassed woman in her late thirties, left the room, grumbling about ill-behaved children and grandmothers who interfere too much. On a happier note, this same grandmother told us another time of the plans she and a neighbor, also an old lady, had made for their grandchildren's marriages. The children in question were all under ten years. "We have it all decided. When Chai-ha grows up she is going to be Kim-tho's wife, and Ge-gou is going to be Cui-chan's wife. If they are all good when they grow up, this is the way we are going to do it: if Kim-tho has more ability than Chai-ha and does better in school, then she will marry into his family, but if she does better, he will marry into our family." The old lady's daughter-in-law was present but did not participate in the conversation. It was quite clear to her that by the time the grandchildren in question were ready to marry, the old ladies would not be around to insist on their plans. A wise daughter-in-law crosses her mother-in-law's bridges when she comes to them.

As long as an older woman retains her health and a fair degree of strength, she is an asset to a busy family. When her daughter-in-law's confinement leaves the household short-handed, she can step in at a minute's notice, picking up familiar routines and running the family as smoothly as she did in years past. Family weddings, major birthdays, funerals, and large religious festivals are events that require a lot of woman power and a good deal of experience. They are considerably easier for the younger woman to handle if she can draw on her mother-in-law's memory of how things were done the last time, or, as frequently happens, if she can hand the management of an event over to her mother-in-law completely. If the special event happens to be in the daughter-in-law's natal family, she enjoys it much more when she can leave all but her youngest child home with her mother-in-law and not have to rush back to put the evening meal on the table. For many a woman in her sixties, this lingering responsibility, the recognition by sons and daughters-in-law of her continued competence, is a source of great satisfaction.

For some women the extra time that comes with retirement as household manager is difficult to fill. Gradually they learn to spend most of the morning washing a few pieces of clothing so they can gossip with the busy women who come down to the river with full baskets. If over the years they have gained a reputation among the village women for their wisdom, they will be much visited for advice on family problems, child-rearing problems, and daughters-in-law who talk back. They may enlarge their personal flock of chickens and ducks, selling them to neighbors or in the morning market in Tapu. Certain women by this time of life have become minor financiers, loaning varying sums of money (at good interest) to friends and friends of friends. In many communities the *hue-a* are nearly dominated by women. *Hue-a* are short-term loan associations that meet well the borrowing needs of a community in which everyone knows everyone else and always has. When someone needs a large sum of money for a wedding or a funeral, he organizes a *hue-a*. If, for example, a man needs NT $8,000, he will invite eight friends to join at NT $1,000 each. At the first meeting, the organizer takes the NT $8,000 and at each of the subsequent meetings (seven in this example) he must pay in the full NT $1,000. In the event someone breaks faith, the organizer is obliged to make up the difference. At the second meeting the members bid for the pot, the lowest bid taking it, and each member putting into the pot the amount that was bid—except of course the organizer, who puts in the full NT $1,000. The next meeting is the same, except that the organizer and the person who took out the second pot must both put in the full NT $1,000. This is a good investment for someone who does not need the lump sum at any particular time, because he can simply wait until the end and take out a full NT $8,000 without having to contribute the full amount except in the first round. The social pressure to fill the obligations contracted by joining these associations is so intense that one rarely hears of a *hue-a* (at least on the village level) collapsing.

It is women of late years who are most likely to make matchmaking an occupation rather than a mere pastime. A woman freed from the responsibilities of meal preparation and child care has the time to make the numerous visits, casual and official, necessary for truly successful matchmaking. If she happens to be a woman with an outgoing personality who has paid careful attention to the various rituals of engagement and marriage, she may find herself with a lively and lucrative business. A talented go-between is in much demand in the country. Although the majority of her business will have to do with marriages, she may also arrange adoptions and settle disputes between family branches, friends, or enemies. In Peihotien there was a very strong-minded old lady in her eighties who hobbled for miles on her tiny bound feet, arranging marriages and adoptions, settling family disputes, and negotiating face-saving compromises for quarrels of various kinds. Her age and her personality commanded respect from even the most arrogant of men, and her tongue lashed the reluctant into submitting to what she considered the best terms they could expect. She was rumored to have an income that exceeded even the earnings of her storekeeping son.

Age and the freedom it brings give some village women the opportunity to become more deeply involved in religious activities. As young mothers they went to the temples only when they had a real need, a sick baby or dying chickens, and as often as not their mothers-in-law were the ones who carried out these errands. Tour groups form around temples to take the believers by bus to the birthday celebrations of some of the important gods on the island. Several middle-aged women from Peihotien visited religious centers in the central and southern parts of the island on more than one occasion, staying for a number of days and stopping with the tour group for some sight-seeing along the way. We witnessed in one family the precise moment when a mother-in-law first realized the possible advantages in the inevitable release of power to her son's wife. A relative invited her to join a bus load of people going on a three-day trip to a festival in Peikang. She had just opened her mouth to refuse automatically when her son suggested that it was years since anyone from their family had visited that particular god. Put in this way, the outing lost its frivolousness and an almost childlike look of temptation crossed her face. It took very little encouragement for her to take the first step into a new phase of her life.

During our stay in Peihotien a major revival of interest in the local Siong-ti-kong (a god) ended in an extensive restoration of his temple. A good many middle-aged women were active in this enterprise, from collecting money for repairs to organizing the final celebration. One old lady who had fussed for years about the lack of attention local people gave to their Siong-ti-kong was particularly gratified. It should be noted that her status as "old lady" made her quite fearless, and she scolded anyone she believed would benefit from it. Siong-ti-kong was not spared one of her tongue-lashings. "Everytime I went there to ask him to protect our family, I told him, 'You are a god of much ability, so why do you just sit there and say nothing? You ought to display your strength and let the people here know what kind of a god you are. It is because you don't display your strength that people here all go elsewhere to *pai-pai*. If you would show your strength, people would all come here!' "

Nearly all religious festivals are accompanied by an outdoor opera or puppet show to entertain both the god and the many people who come to worship him. Before the introduction of television, these performances were the most popular form of entertainment in the countryside. Movies attracted the young and to a lesser extent the older generation, but the operas and the puppet shows attracted everyone. Just as many American women become addicted to soap operas, many Taiwanese women become addicted to folk opera. Some women walk for miles on a hot day to see the afternoon performance,

225

walk home to get some dinner, and then go back for the long evening session. Those who are lucky enough to be no longer burdened with the responsibility of a household follow this schedule as long as a cycle of operas continues. The stories are old and familiar, the costumes often shabby, and the sound from the loudspeakers frequently deafening and unintelligible. But for women who cannot read, or who find little to read if they can, this escape into fantasy for a few hours is delightful. With the advent of television and the presence today of a set in virtually every house in the Taipei basin, the opera and puppet shows are more popular than ever. The difference is that the performances now drawing the biggest crowds are the ones on television. On our last visit we found it impossible to do any interviewing during the hours that puppet shows or Taiwan opera are being telecast. A foreigner cannot compete with the drawing power of local drama televised.

One of the less happy activities that attracts older women is gambling. Everyone, young or old, gambles a bit at New Year, and a woman home for a visit with free time will play a game of mah-jong or cards, but for some women who find themselves completely free of domestic responsibilities, gambling becomes an exciting as well as a sociable way to pass every afternoon. Unfortunately, the countryside is full of professional or semiprofessional gamblers who patiently cheat the old ladies out of their stakes. Even if they manage to stay in fairly "friendly" games, gambling is usually a losing proposition and may be a very expensive pastime. One dear old lady who lived in Peihotien gambled away so much of the family savings before the extent of her debts was discovered that her two sons faced a financial crisis. Every morning she promised not to gamble but by nightfall she had always managed to slip off to join a game. Her family finally had to send her to live with her eldest son in Keelung, a comfortless city where she knew no one and would not be tempted into gambling for a while. The most severely addicted gamblers among the women are those who worked for any period of time as prostitutes. Gambling was one of the skills of their profession. They learned to play for high stakes—often with someone else's money. In their old age, the habit returns to haunt them, at great cost to their children and to their own peace of mind.

Considering the rigors of life in rural Taiwan—the heavy humid summers that breed a variety of ills, the damp cold winters in unheated houses that leave most of the population coughing and sneezing, the high incidence of tuberculosis, the reluctance to spend money on expensive medical treatment, the cycles of crop failure, poverty, and poor nutrition, the excessive number of childbirths, and the overwork—it is amazing how many fragile old ladies of eighty or more one finds in the villages of the Taipei basin. They may have just enough strength to dress themselves and hobble outdoors to chat with similarly worn-out neighbors or talk with visiting anthropologists, but unlike their pathetic husbands, they are not considered drones in a busy farm family until they are completely bedridden. Although slow, they can still help wash vegetables for supper or tend a fretful infant, jobs that an old man has never done and would not know how to handle at this late age. This fact was pointed out to us by an old, old lady with a smile of bitter triumph. She also pointed out how many more old ladies there were around than old men.

But finally there comes a morning when a child has to be sent to see why grandmother is sleeping so late, to call her to eat her congee while it is still warm enough to take the chill from her bones. The little girl returns with a queer look of fear and uncertainty on her face. Within a few hours the house is a hubbub of activity, relatives pouring in to help with plans for the funeral and neighbors dropping by to offer help and advice. Arguments rise and fall over who should do what, which relatives should be summoned, how much should be spent, and where that much cash can be raised. The women clothe the old lady in the funeral finery she probably prepared herself. When all is ready, the coffin, which she may also have bought herself, is brought before the ancestral altar, and she is lowered into it, along with packets of ritual money and other items of use to her in her journey. Here she will rest, in the center of the family, until the day set by the geomancer as auspicious for her funeral. In the evening when the various relatives and neighbors have left and the ritual wailing has ceased, her son may sit for a while in the main hall, staring at her coffin and remembering, not so much the little old lady who died that morning, but gentle hands on a cut knee, warm comfort after a midnight terror, a safe refuge from sure punishment, special bits of food when family rations were low, soft black eyes silently expressing their pride in him. All of the day's advice about economizing here and there, since it is only a woman who died, will be dismissed in those few minutes. The son will not be so indiscreet as to have a more elaborate funeral than the one he staged for his father, but he will once again bring the family into a year of hard times to provide his mother with a funeral that will make her proud. He owed it to his father—but he cannot bring himself not to provide it for his mother. And when the day arrives, he will feel somewhat easier about the impatience of the last few years when he was so busy and she so querulous. He will watch with pride as the long file of mourners, clad in burlap and muslin relieved with bright patches of red and blue, follows the coffin through the brilliant rice paddies to the mountains. Her soul will be carried back in a tablet and placed on the family altar, irrevocably at last an official member of the family. That evening (after a huge feast) elaborate, entertaining, and expensive rituals will be staged by Taoist priests to see another part of her soul through the various levels of the underworld, bribing officials, paying tolls, and fending off spirits. In the days that follow, the son will dutifully burn incense to his mother, morning and evening—but in time he will turn the duty over to his wife.

Index

Index

233

Index

Filial obligation, 14–15, 17, 25, 31, 156–57, 192, 216–17
Friendship, importance of women's, 38–39, 42–52, 75, 146–47
Funerals, 11, 216, 228–29

Gambling, 82–83, 110, 168, 226–27
Go-betweens, 106–7, 114, 223–24
Gods, 10f, 55, 82, 141, 150–51, 153, 224f
Grandparent and grandchild relations, 72–73, 75, 164, 221–22

Hue-a (loan associations), 223
Husband and wife relations, 111, 137, 140–46 *passim*, 157, 160–63, 168–69, 195–96, 220

Incest, 23, 181–83
Infanticide, 54
Infants, 53–62, 73, 158

Joint Commission on Rural Reconstruction, 6f

Koxinga (Cheng Ch'eng-kung), 2–3
Kuan-im (a goddess), 150–51
Kui khi, 63–64, 154–55
Kui mia:, 63–64

Liu Ming-chuan, 4–5
Loan associations (*hue-a*), 223

Mainlanders, defined, 8
Marriage: men who make uxorilocal, 17, 192, 193–94, 198–99, 204, 205–6; major, 18, 171; advantages of *sim-pua*, 18, 173, 178–79, 189–90; young people's dislike of *sim-pua*, 23, 180–90; "love" type, 101–5 *passim*, 108, 112–16 *passim*, 145–46; women's attitude toward uxorilocal, 192–93, 195–96, 204, 205–6; consensual, 201f

Menstruation, 57, 94–96
Mother and daughter relations, 67–68, 79, 105, 111–12, 131–33, 139–40
Mother and son relations, 67–68, 79, 160–63, 204, 228–29
Mother-in-law and daughter-in-law: in uterine family, 35f, 132, 149–51, 152, 158–60; in women's community, 39–40, 146–47; relations between, 104, 125–26, 129–30, 133, 219–20; during honeymoon period, 142–44, 165–66; and transfer of power, 163–64, 167–68, 218–19, 221–22; in *sim-pua* marriages, 173, 178–80, 189–90

Nurturance training, 73–74

Obedience training, 65–66, 67, 78–79, 94
Opera, folk, 225–26

Peihotien, described, 8–9, 10, 12
Placenta God (Thai-sin), 153
Pollution, ritual, 56–57, 95–96
Pregnancy, 63, 137, 152–55
Prostitution, 98–99, 205–14
Pu-hsi-pan (tutoring system), 90ff

Quarrels, adult, 30, 46–47, 74–75, 180

Sanhsia, described, 10–13
Schools, 22, 67, 80–95, 100
Sex, attitudes toward, 129, 139–40
Sexual segregation, 62, 80, 96–97, 100, 130
Shaman (*tang ki*), 149–50
Sibling order, 61–62, 109–10, 143–44
Sim-pua, 16–17, 18, 23, 172–85, 189–90
Siong-ti-kong (a god), 225
Siou tia: (bride price), 103, 115, 118–21
Sisters, relations between, 34

234

Index

235